J.A. CULICAN

art by ARNILD ALDEPOLLA

KEEPER OF DRAGONS

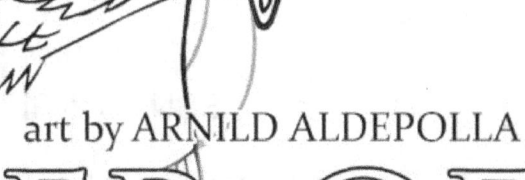
THE COLORING BOOK

Illustrations by: Arnild Aldepolla

Story by: J.A. Culican

ISBN 10: 1717310958

ISBN-13: 978-1717310958

Dragon Realm Press

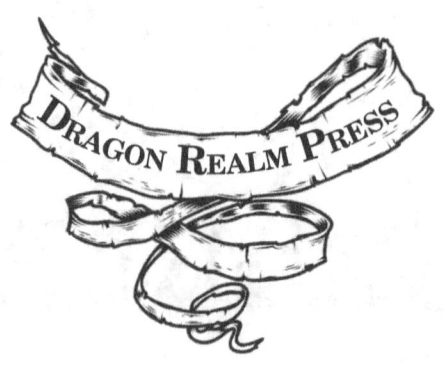

THE PRINCE RETURNS

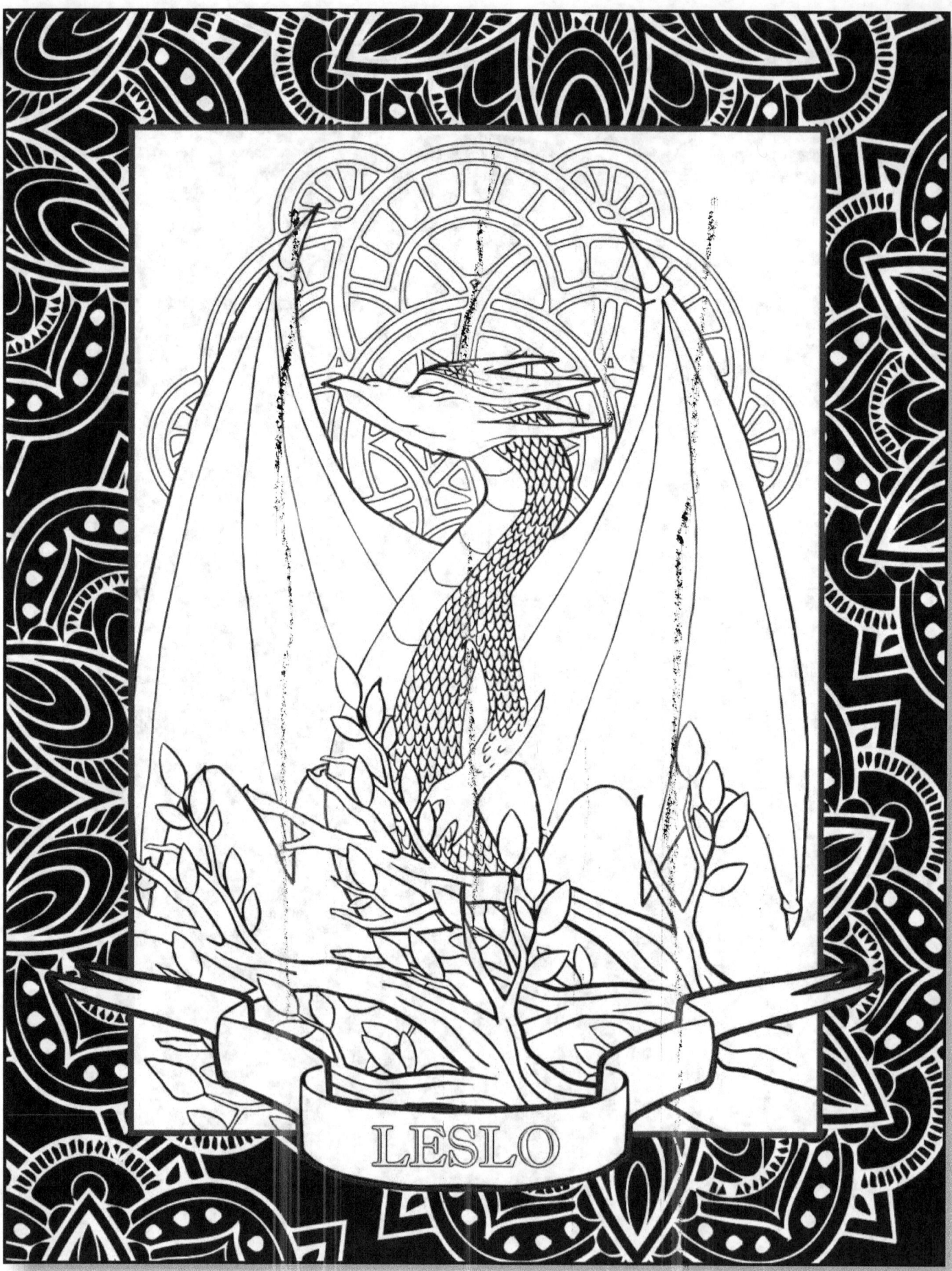

LESLO

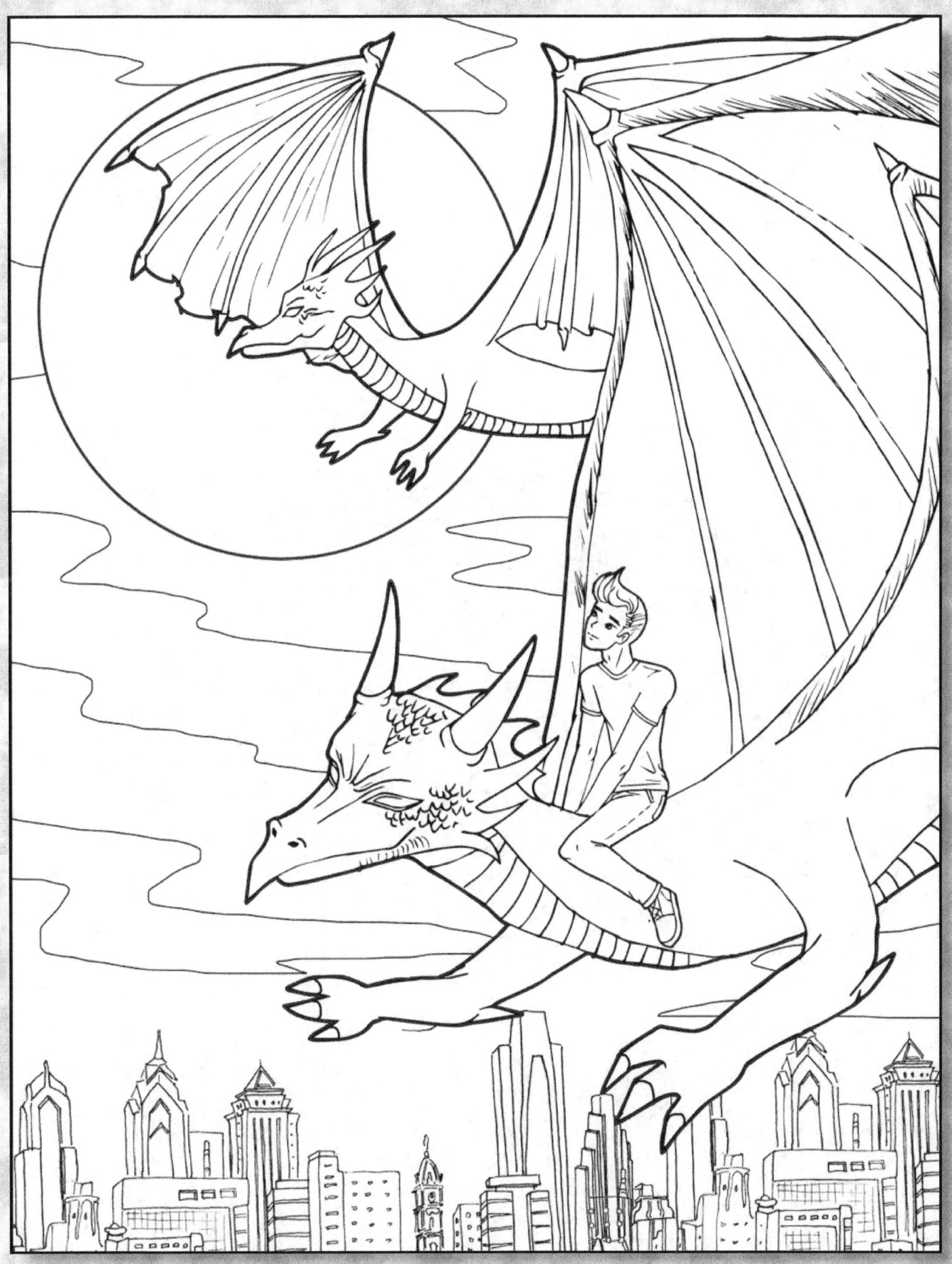

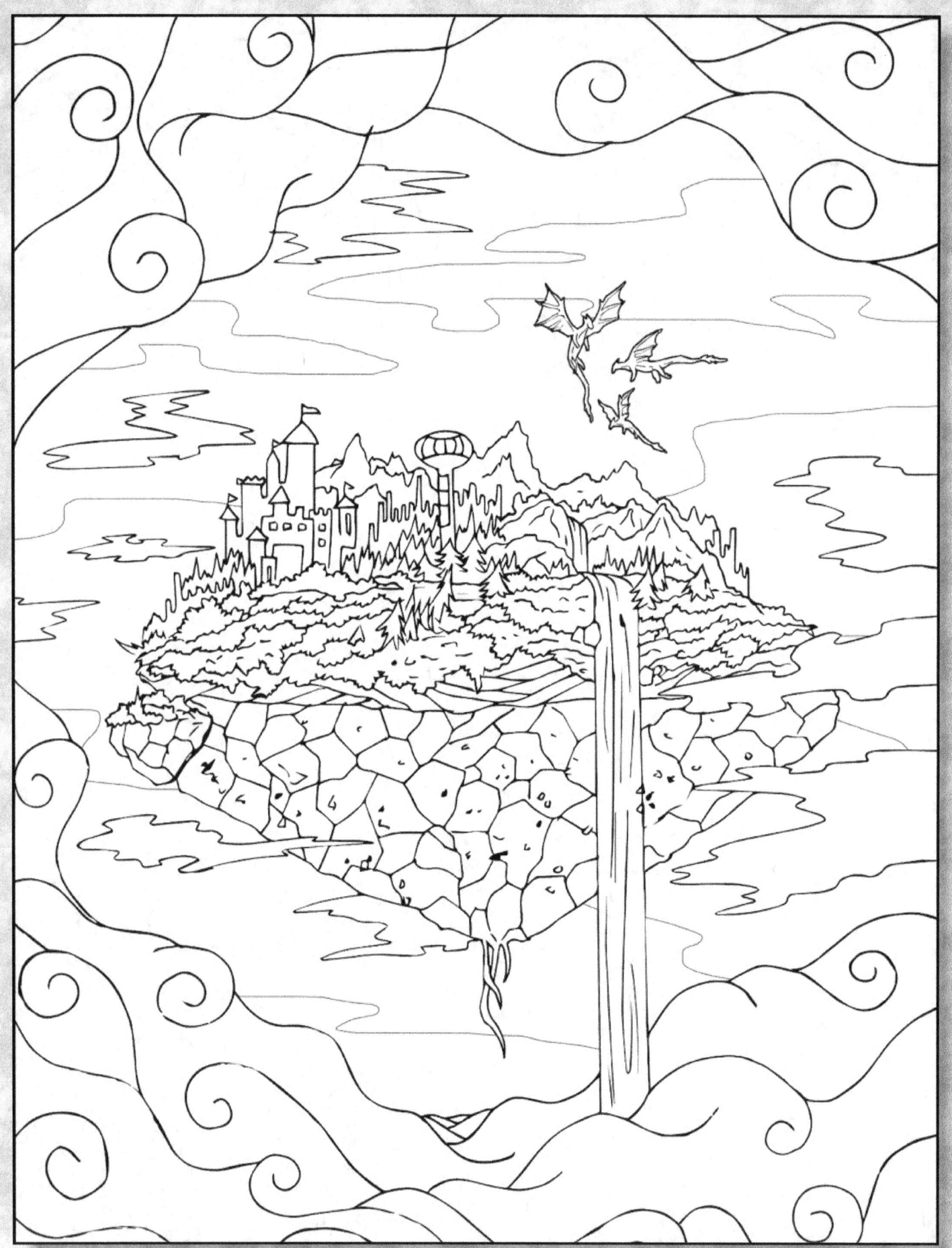

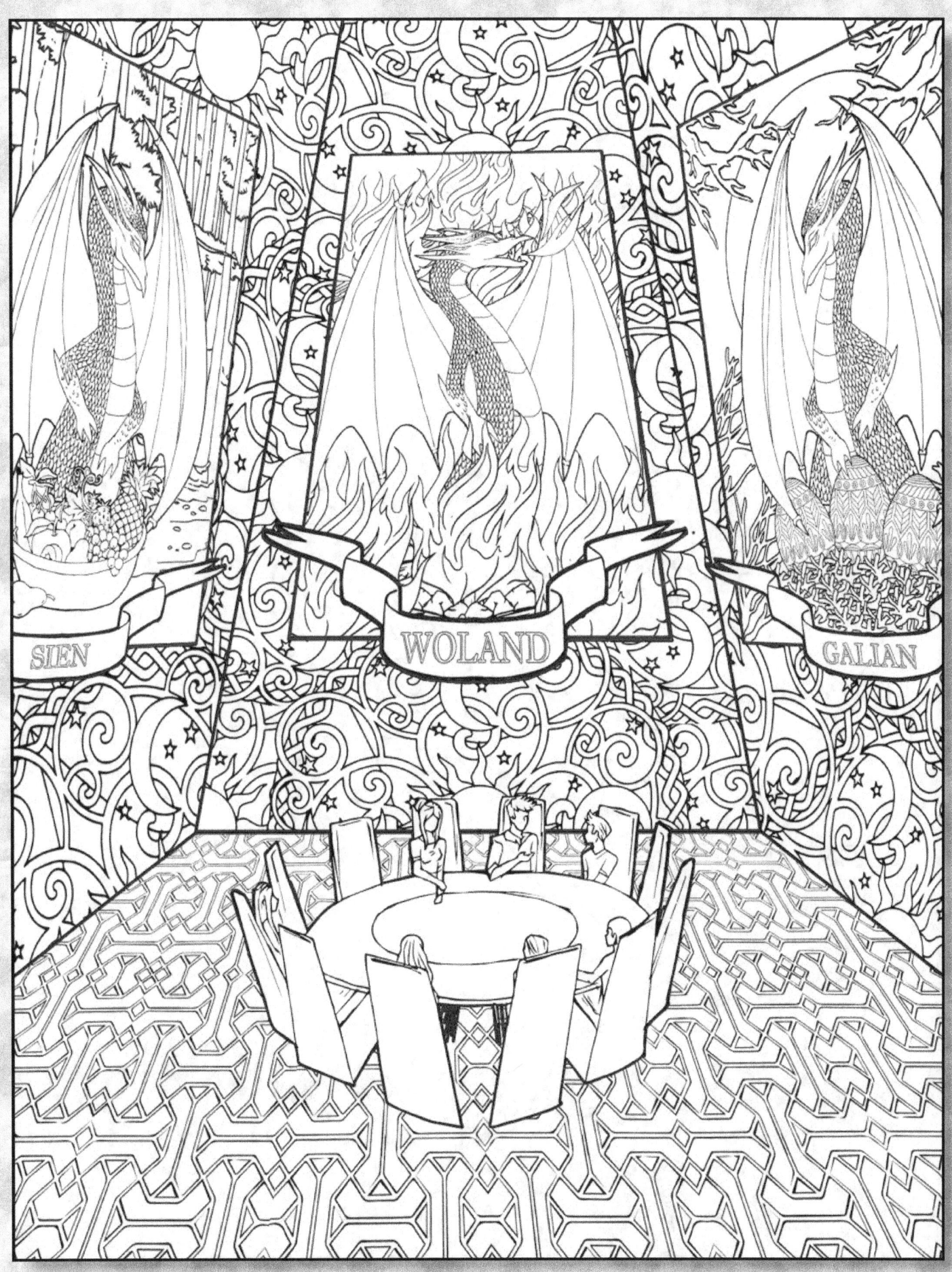

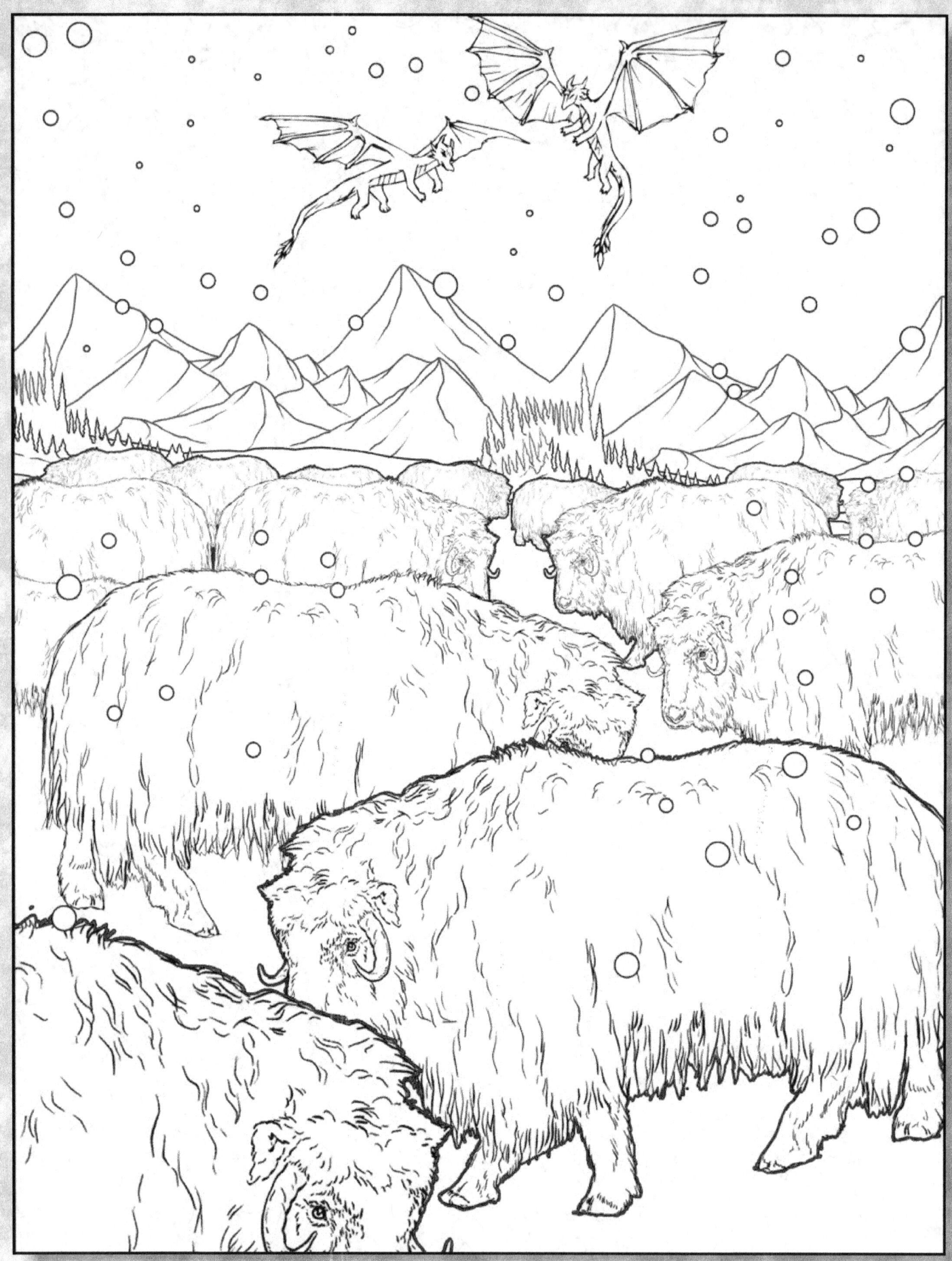

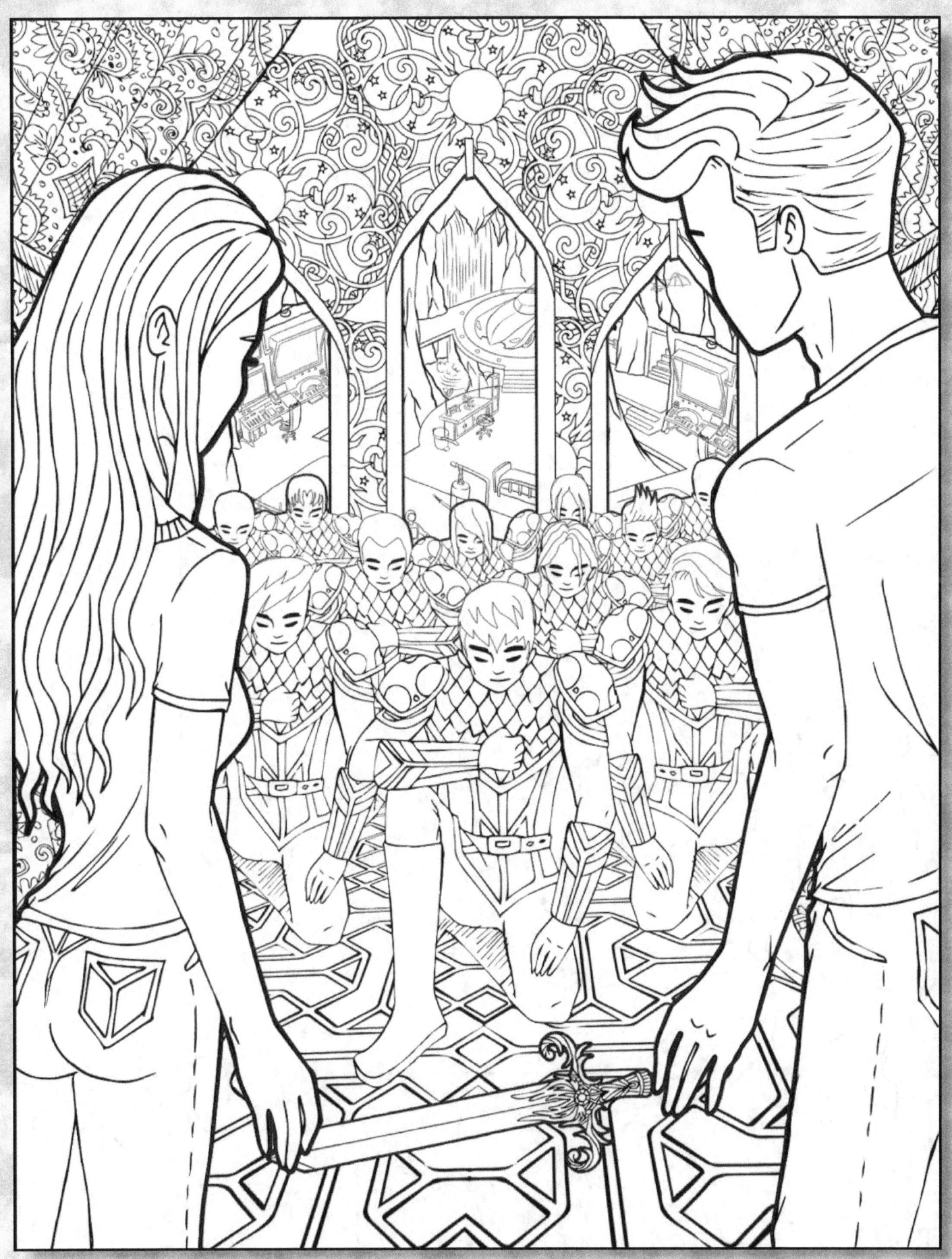

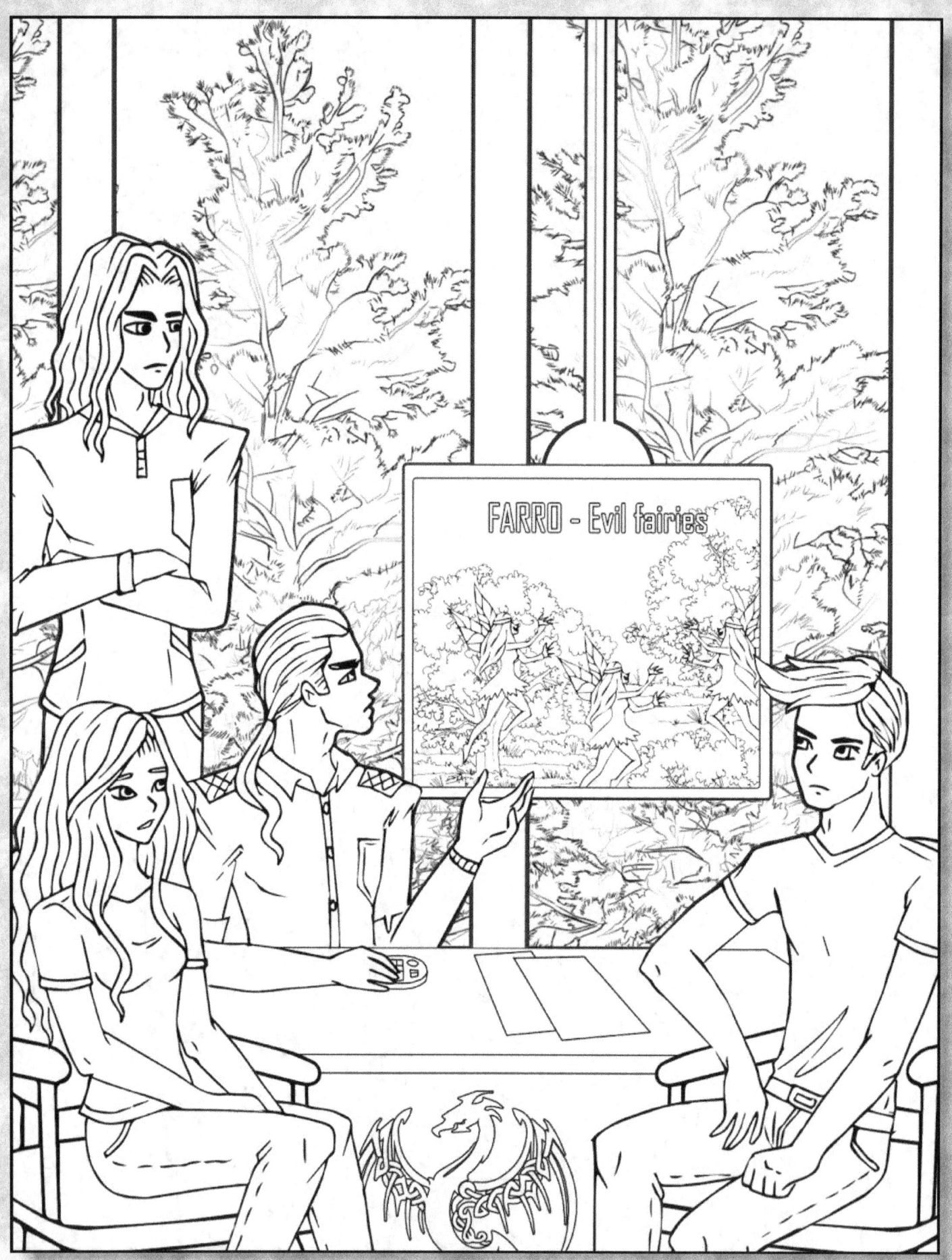

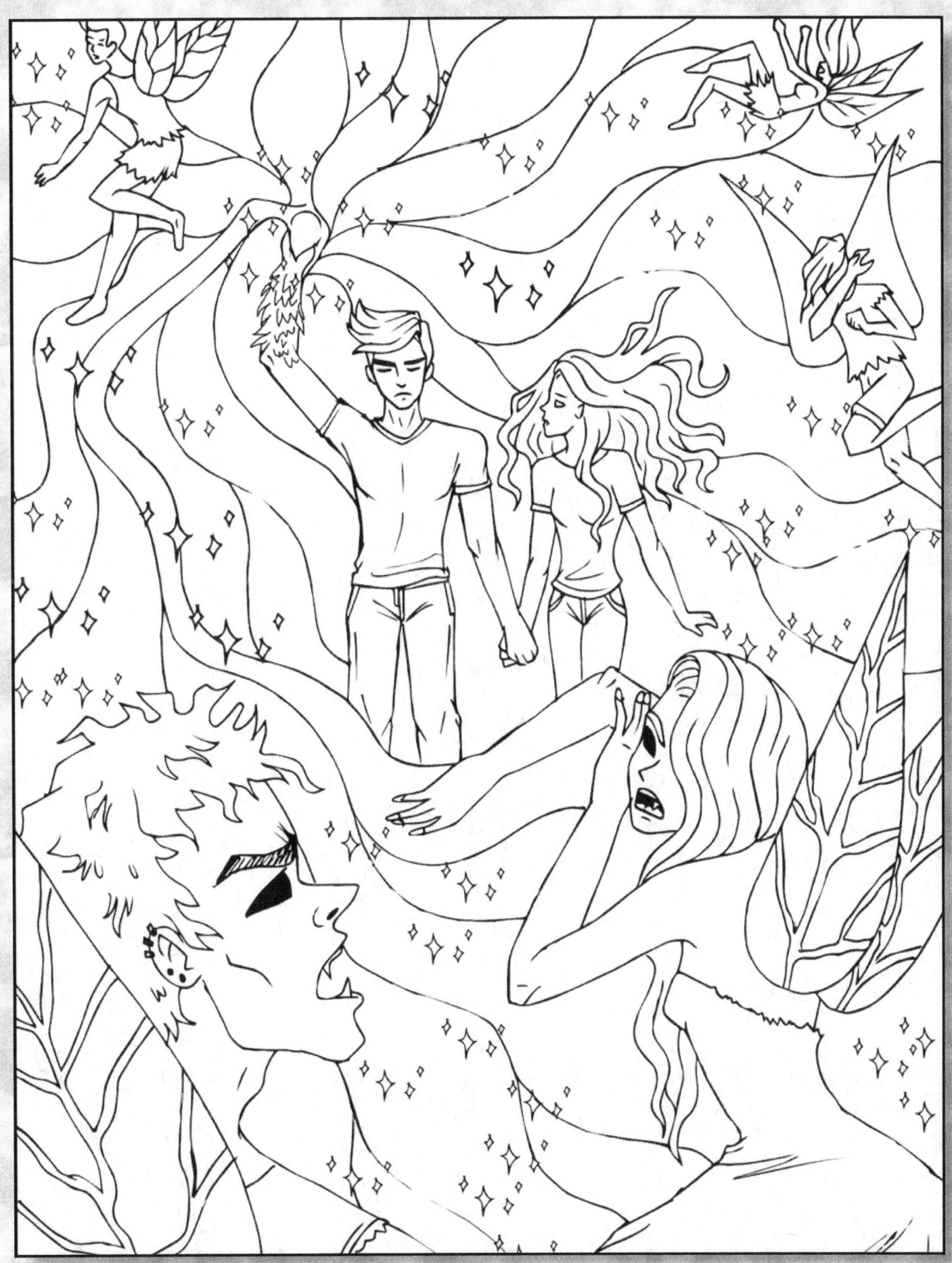

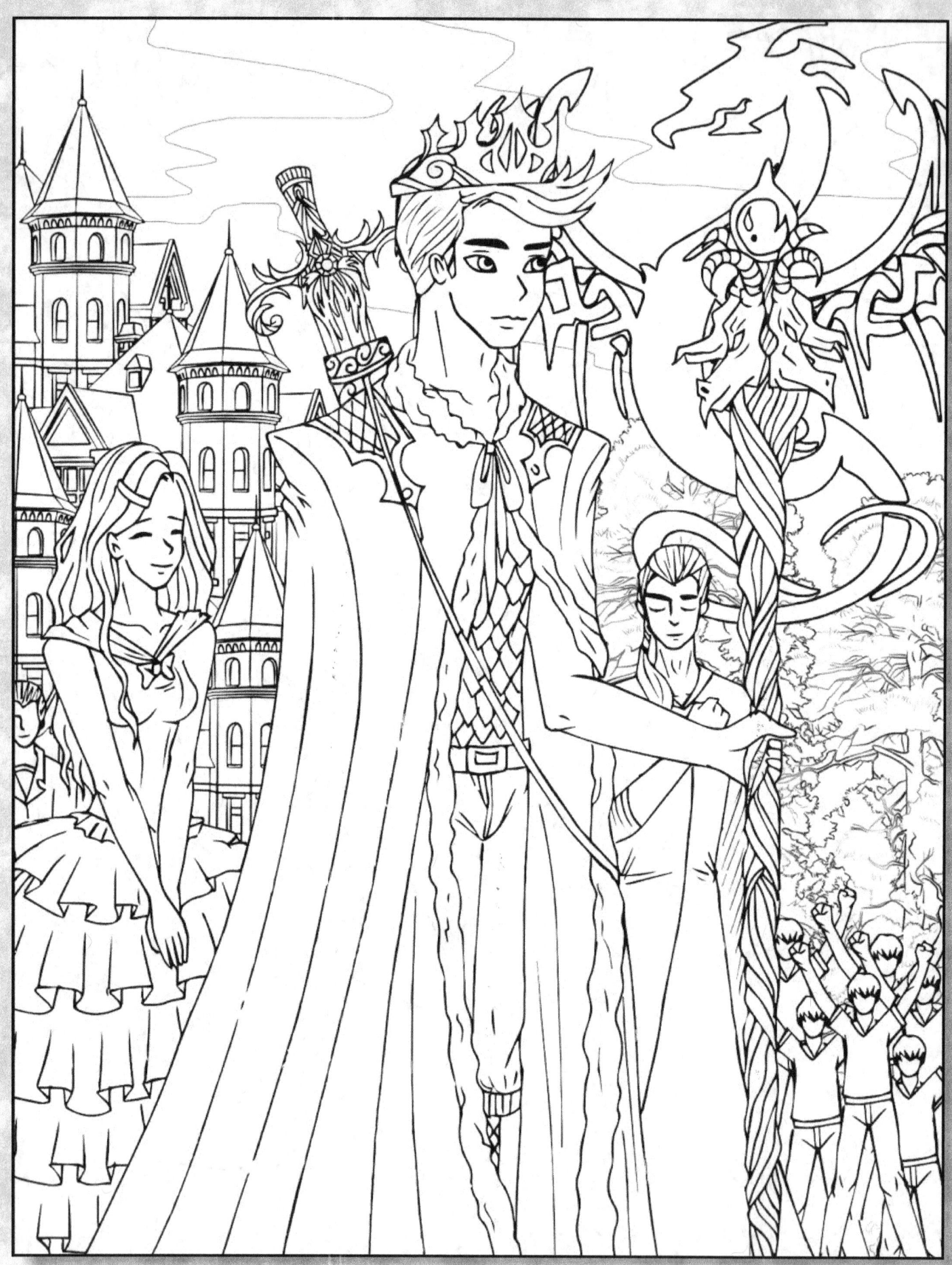

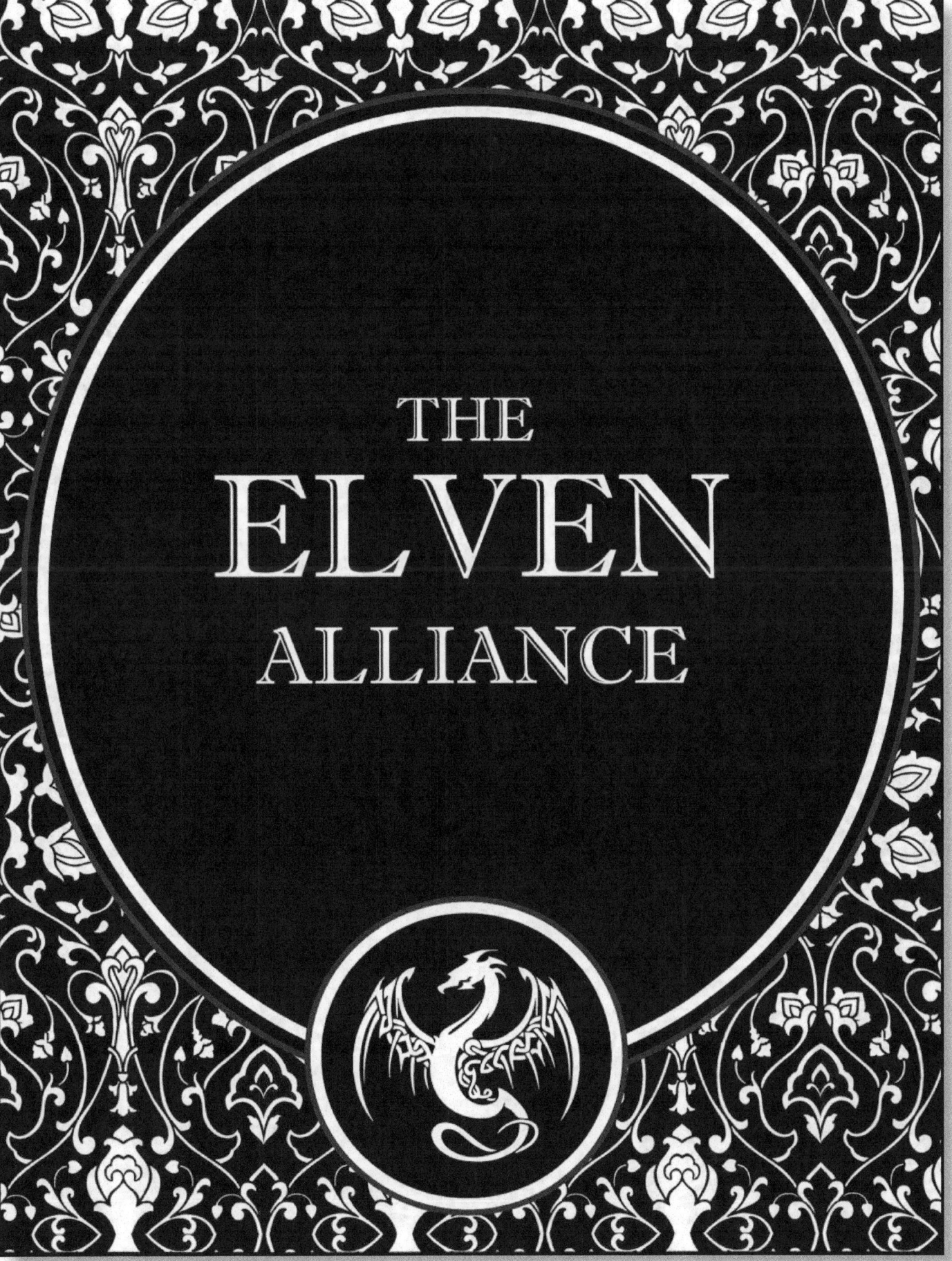

THE
ELVEN
ALLIANCE

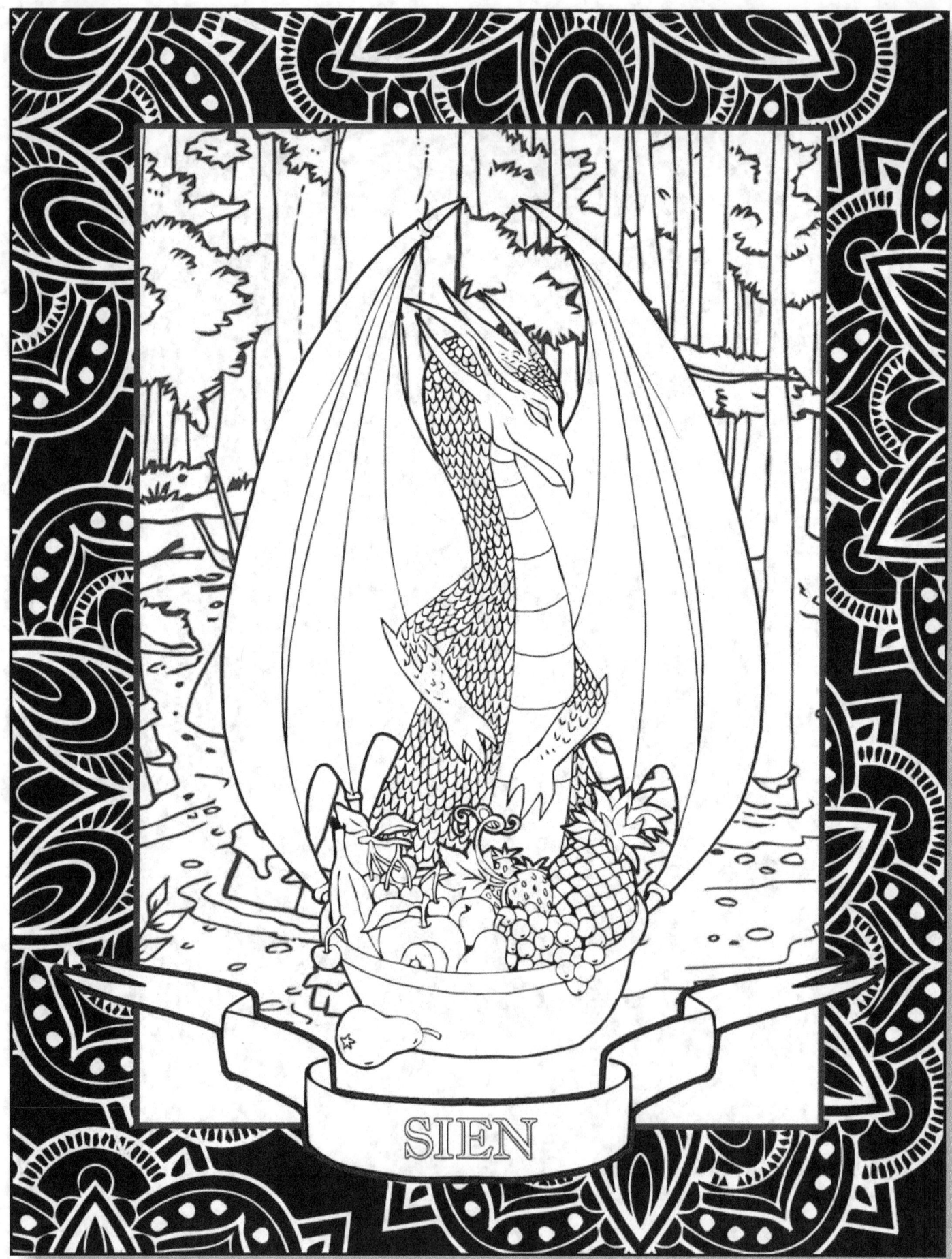

SIEN

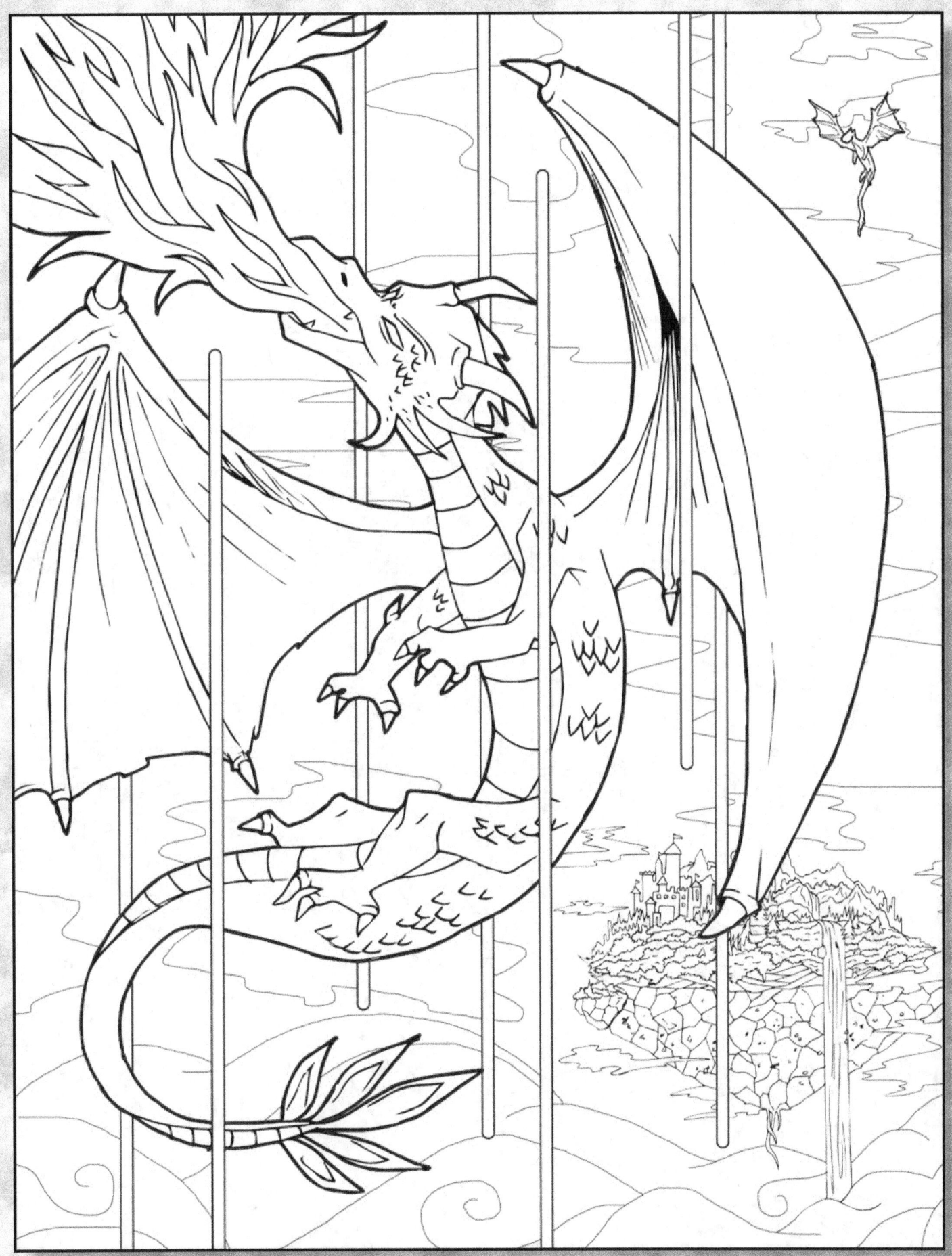

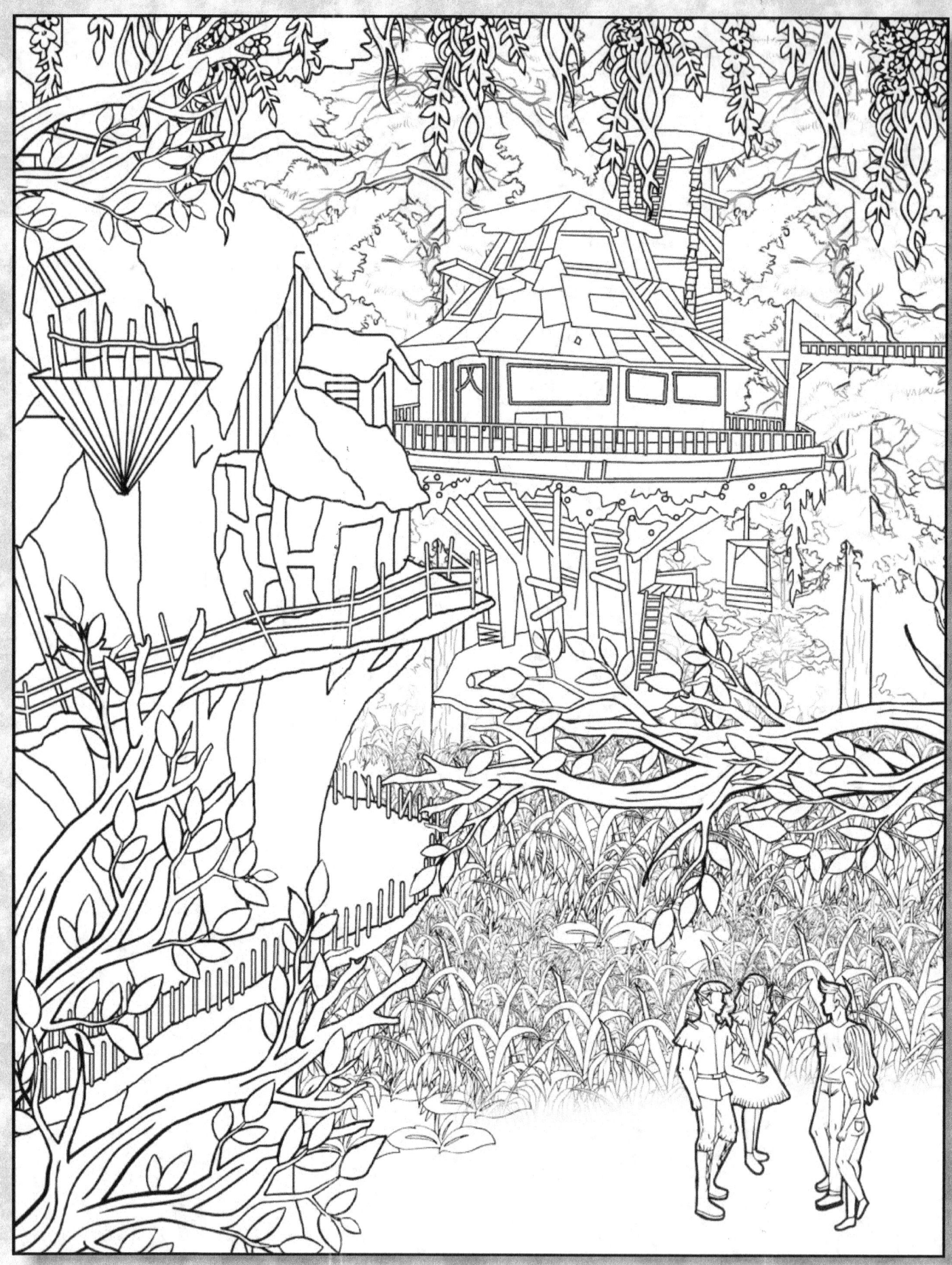

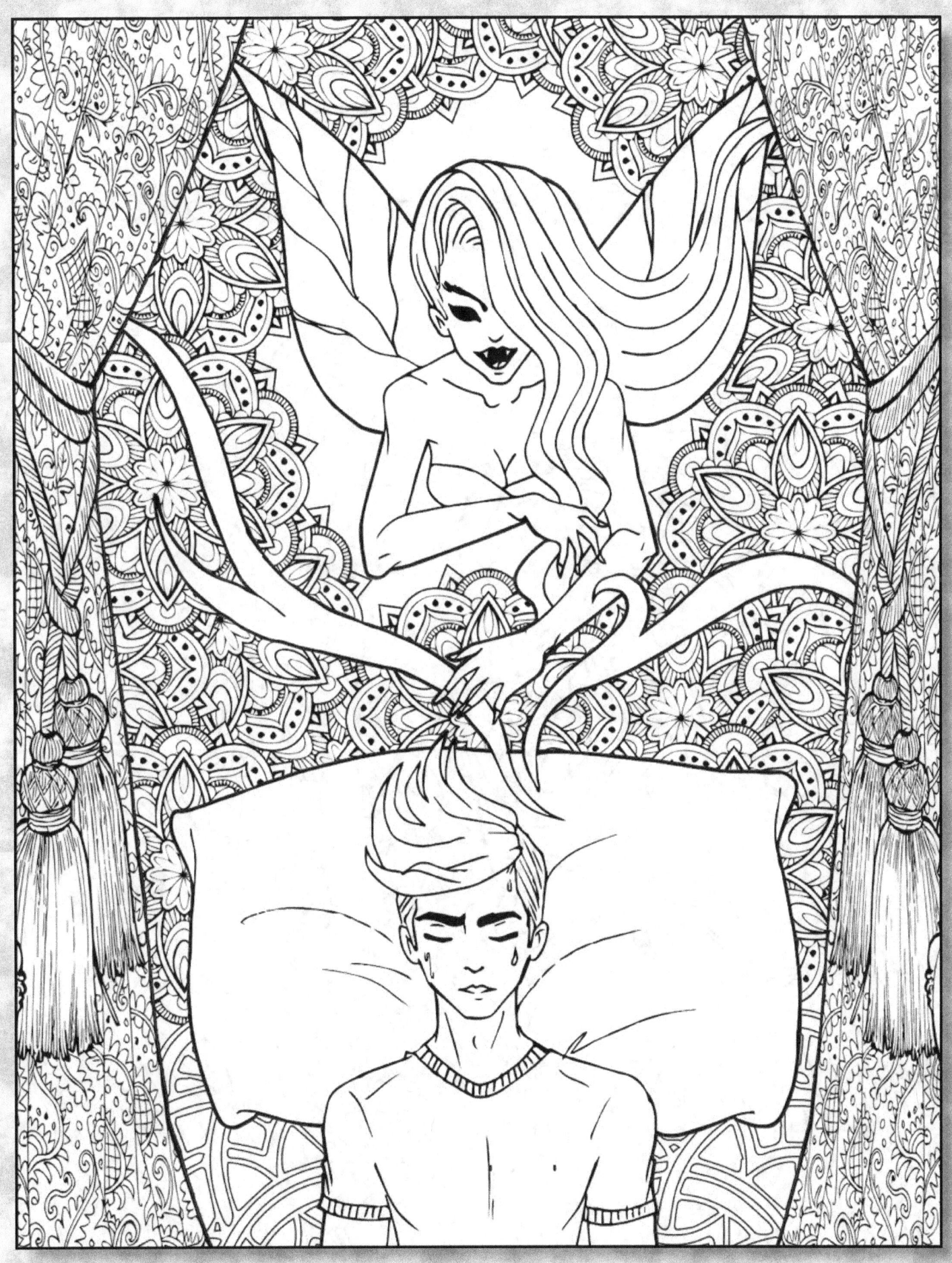

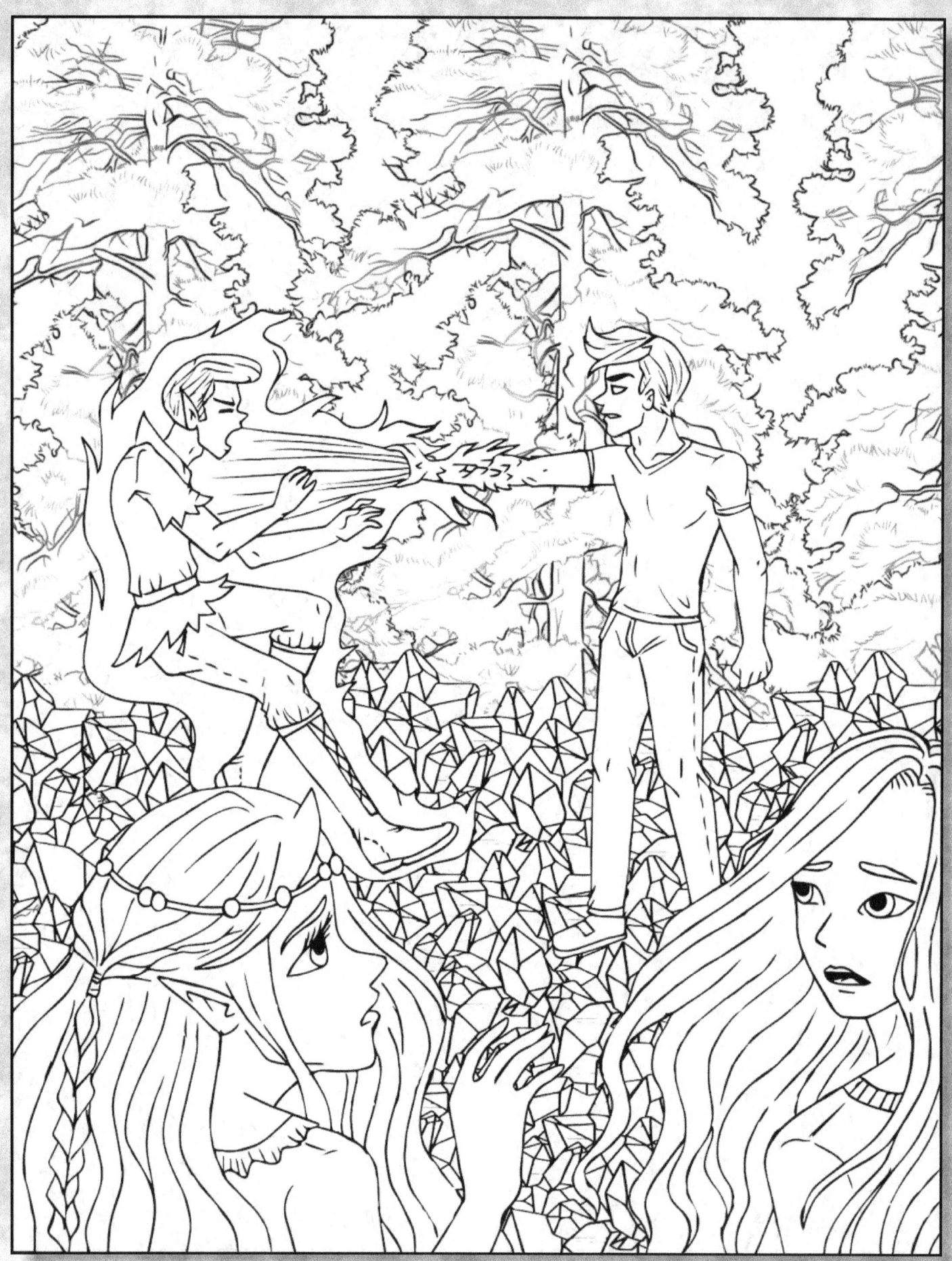

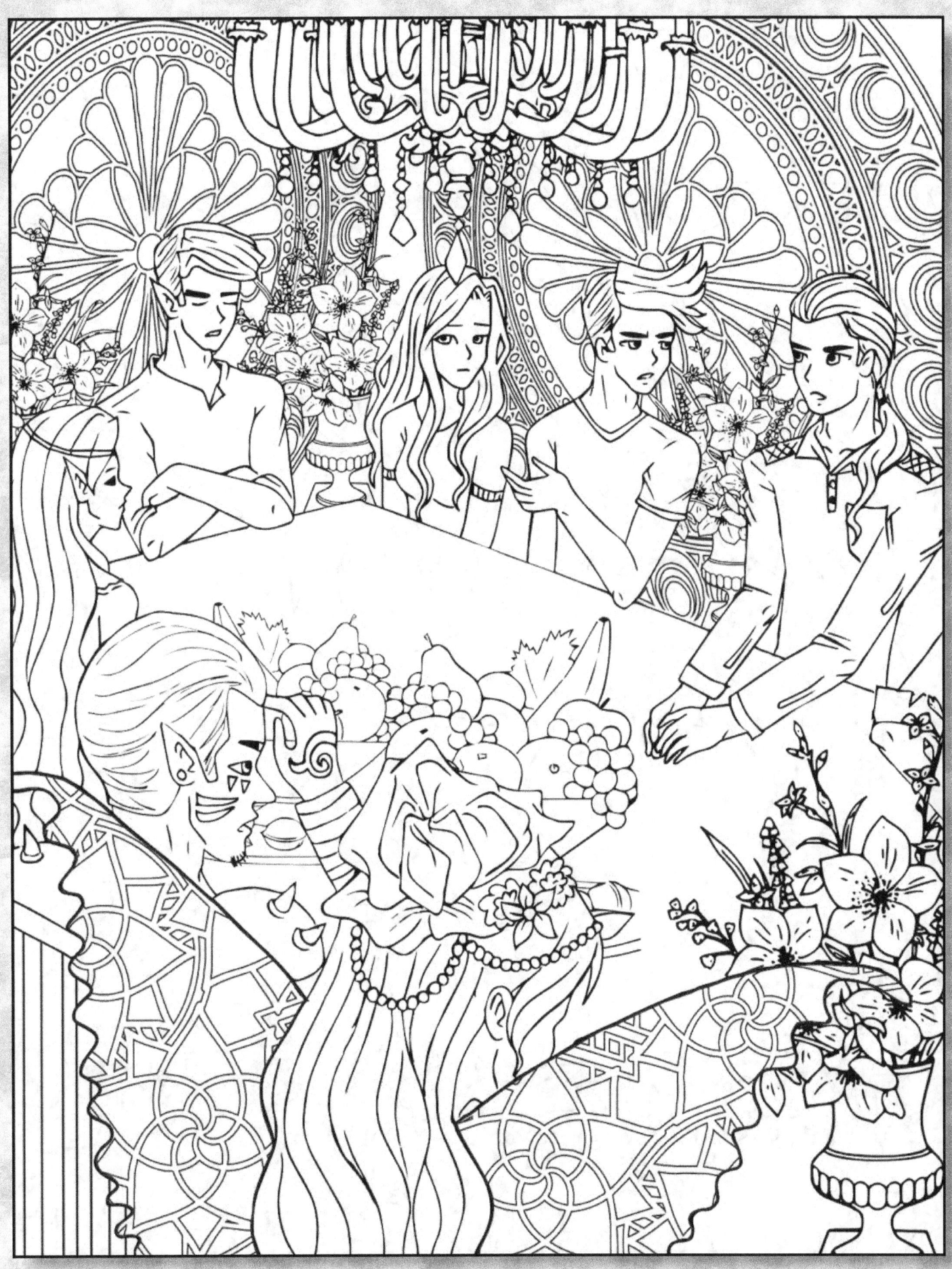

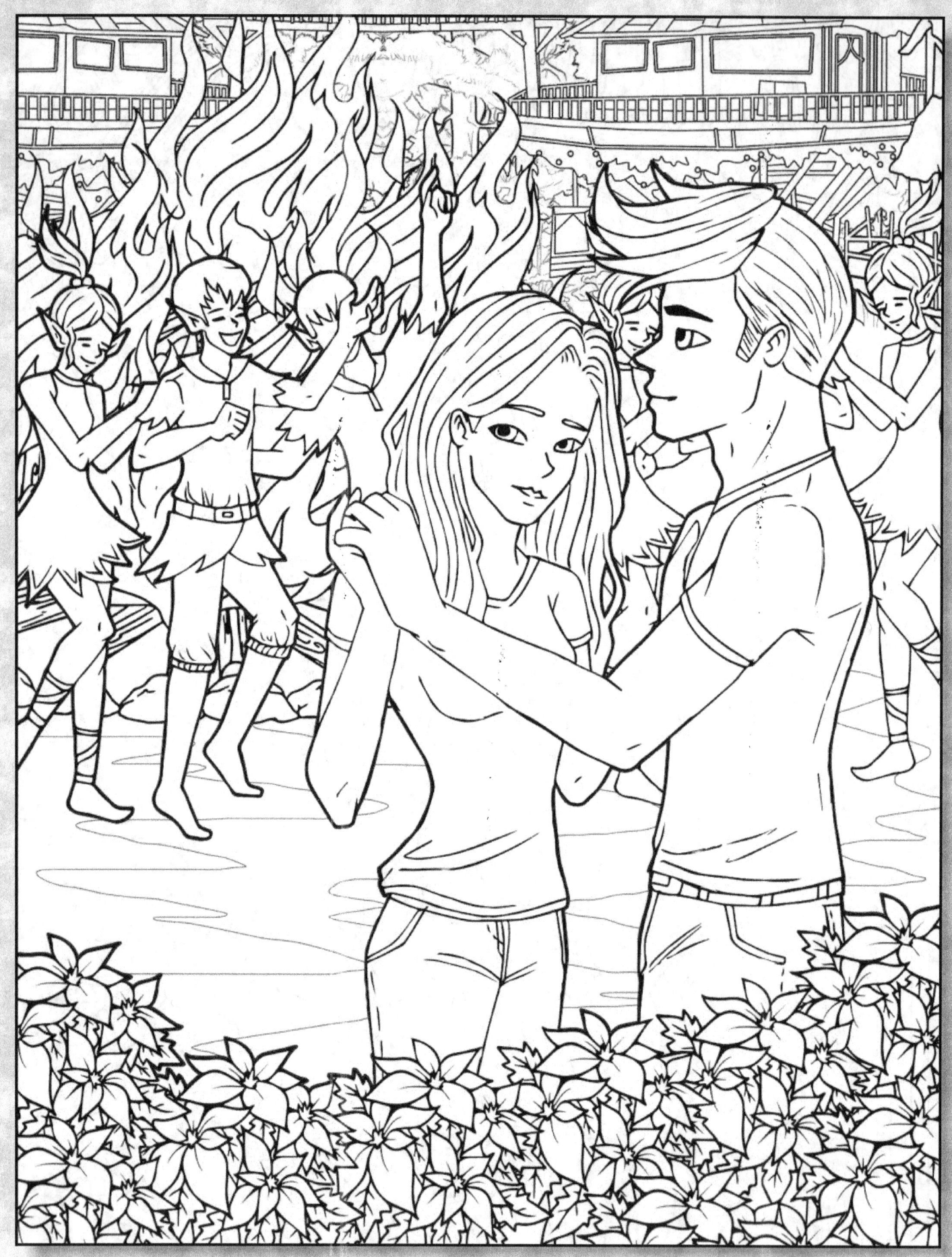

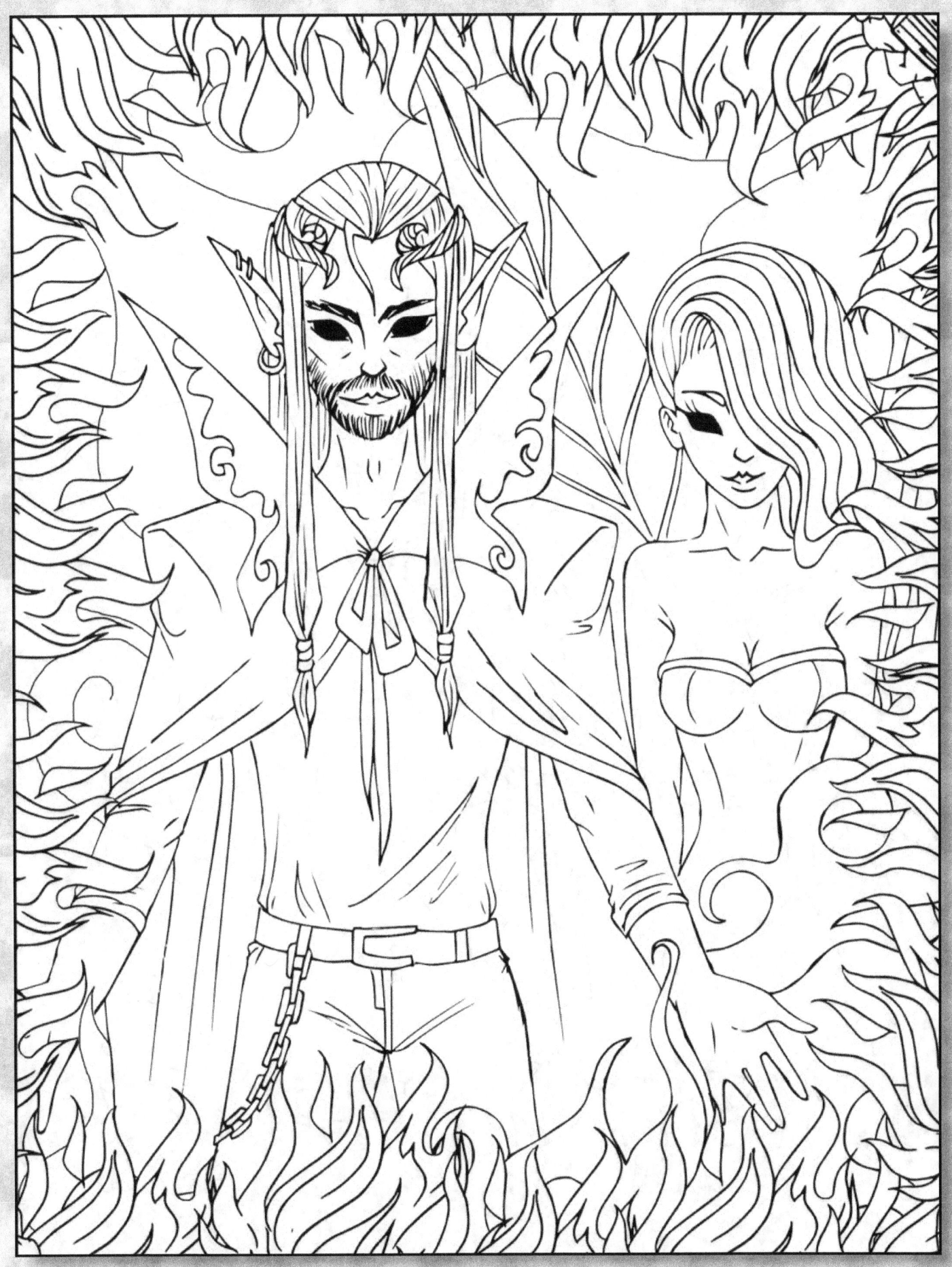

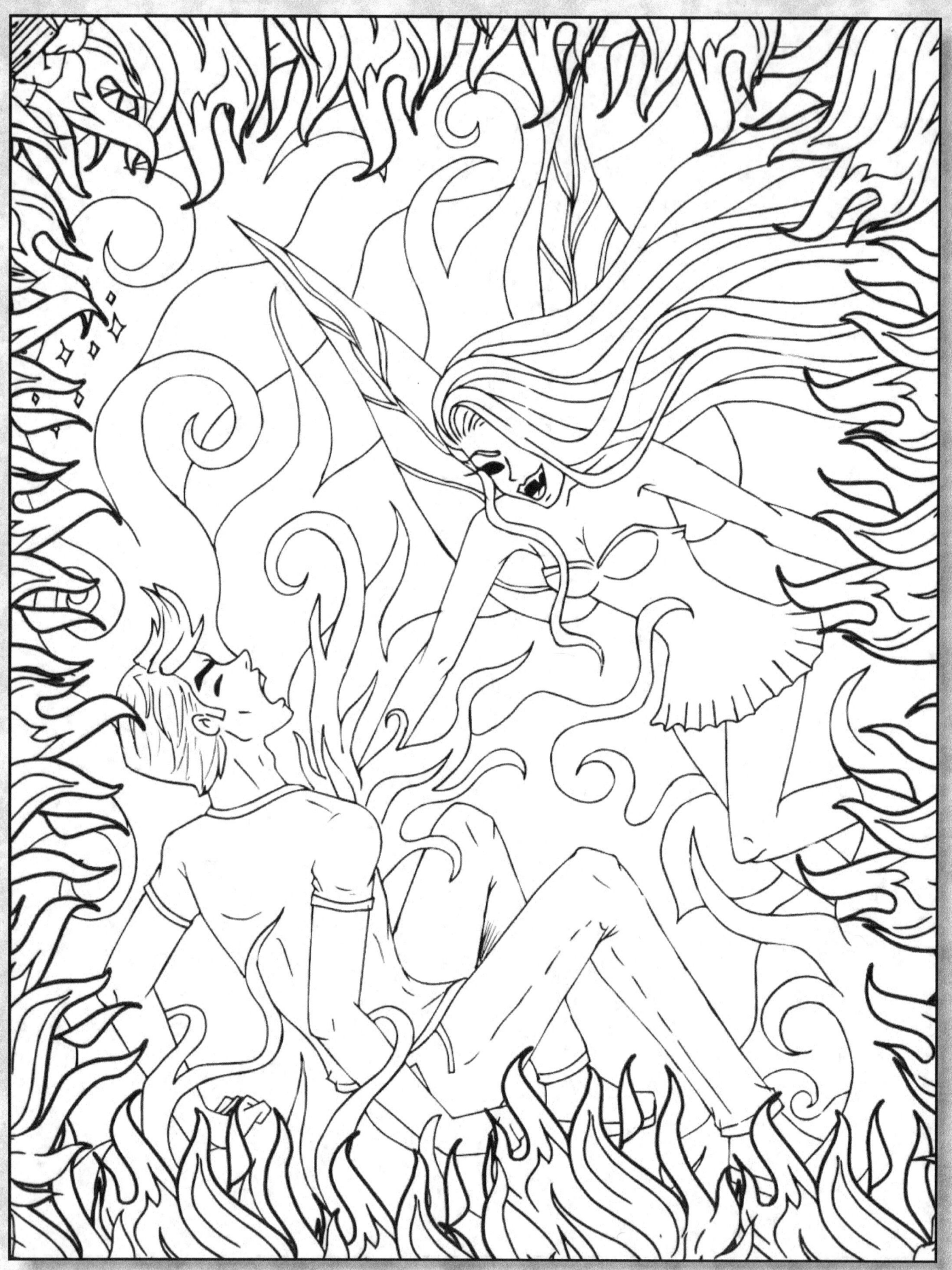

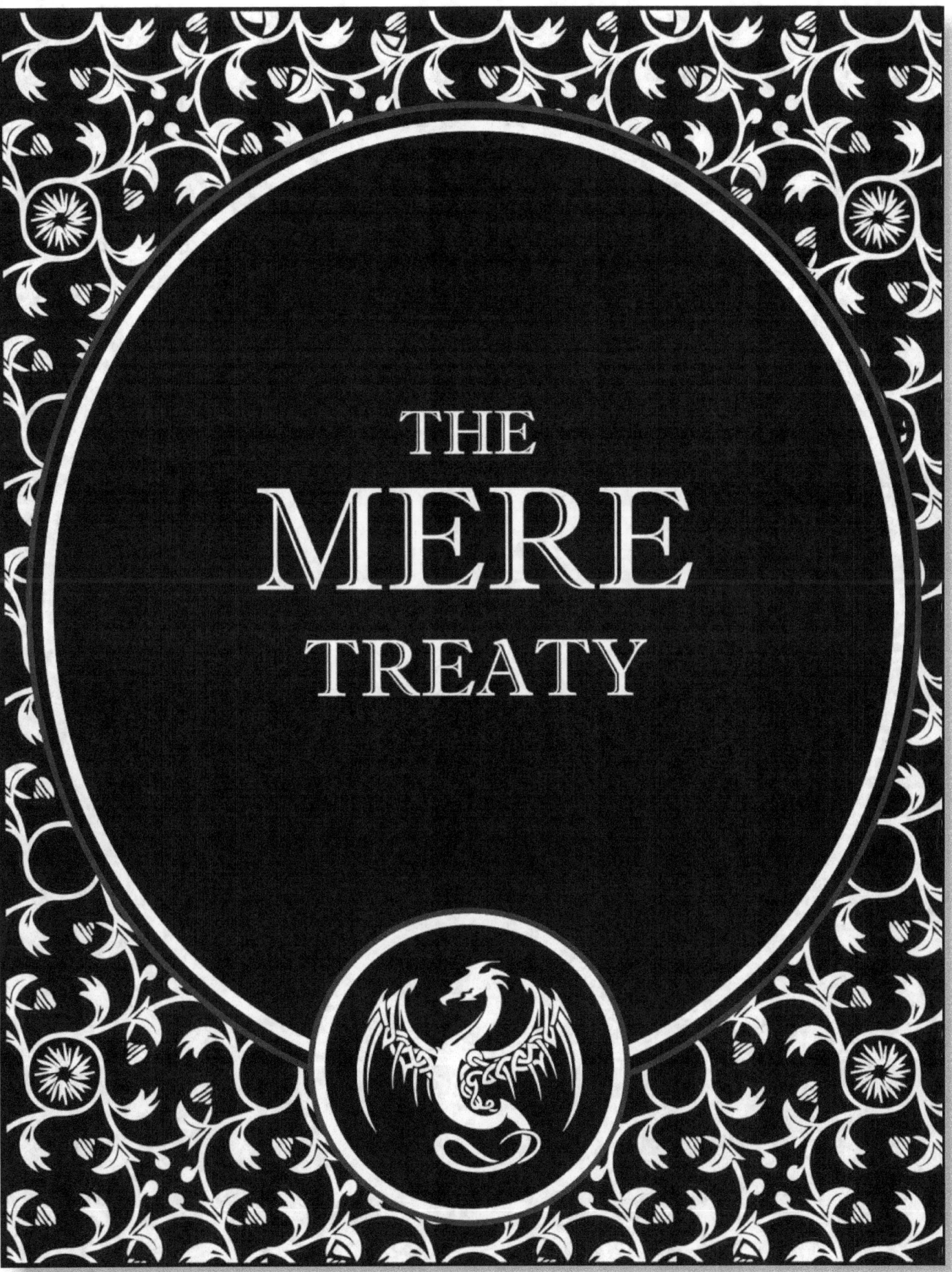

THE
MERE
TREATY

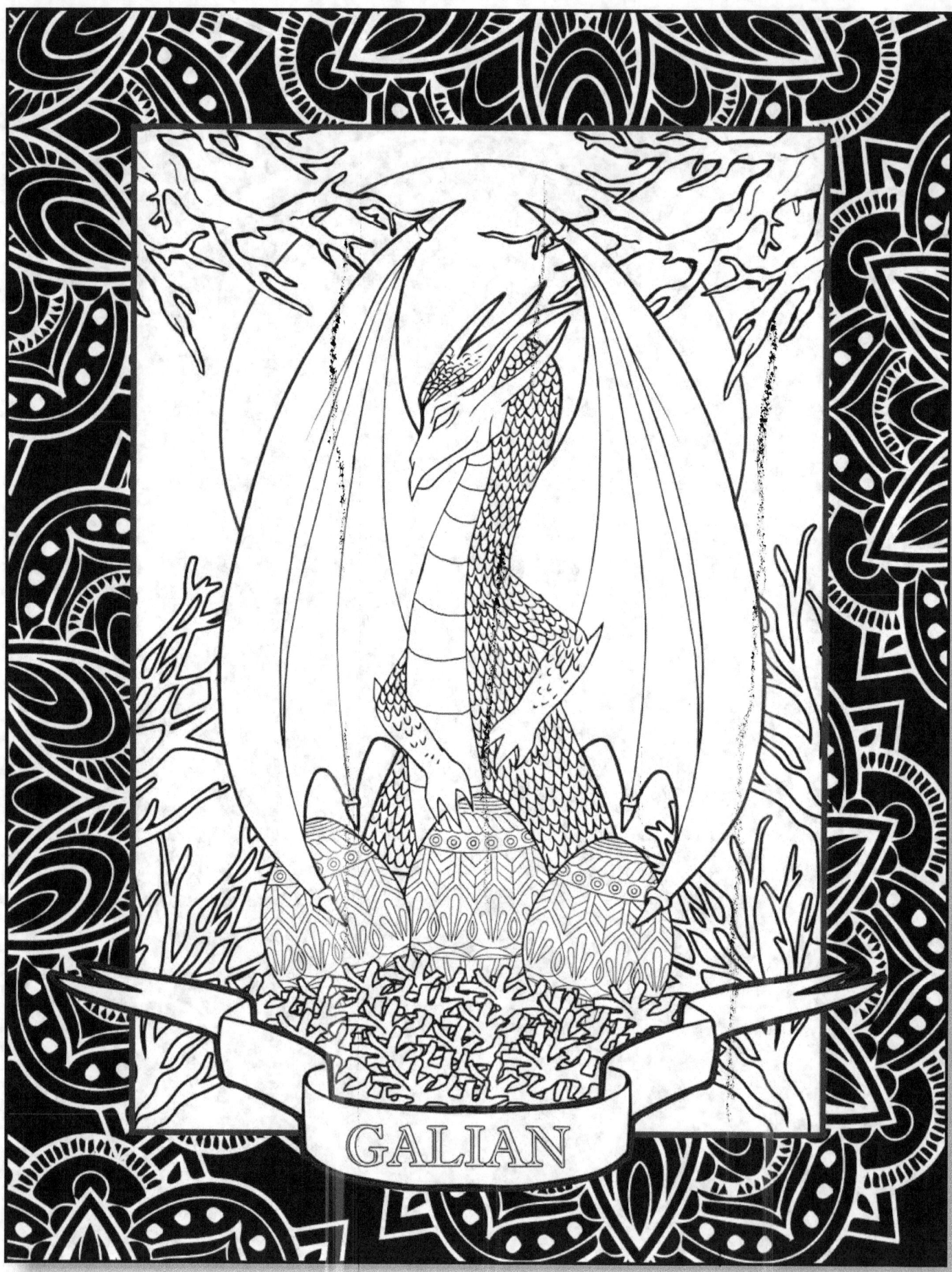

GALIAN

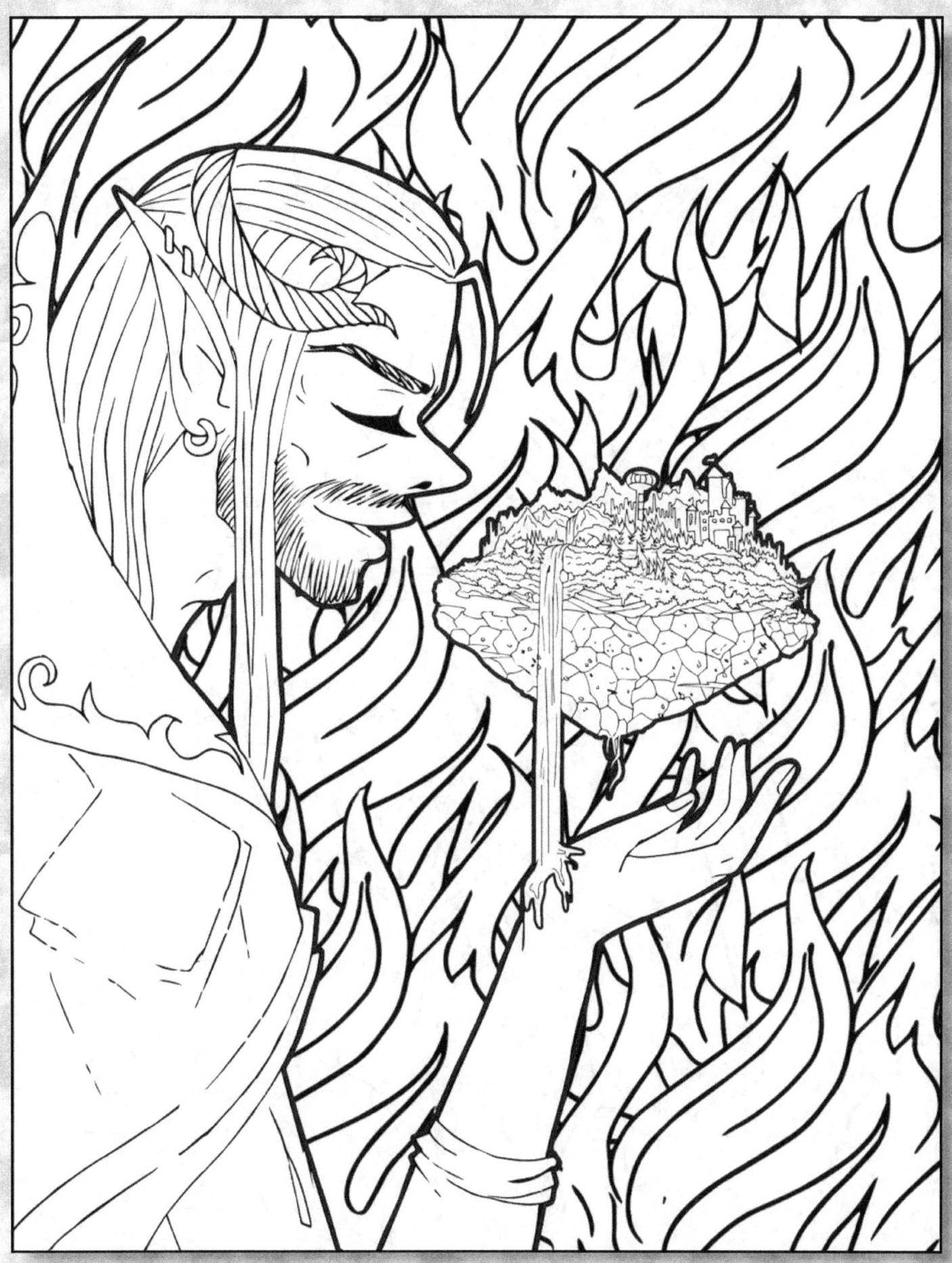

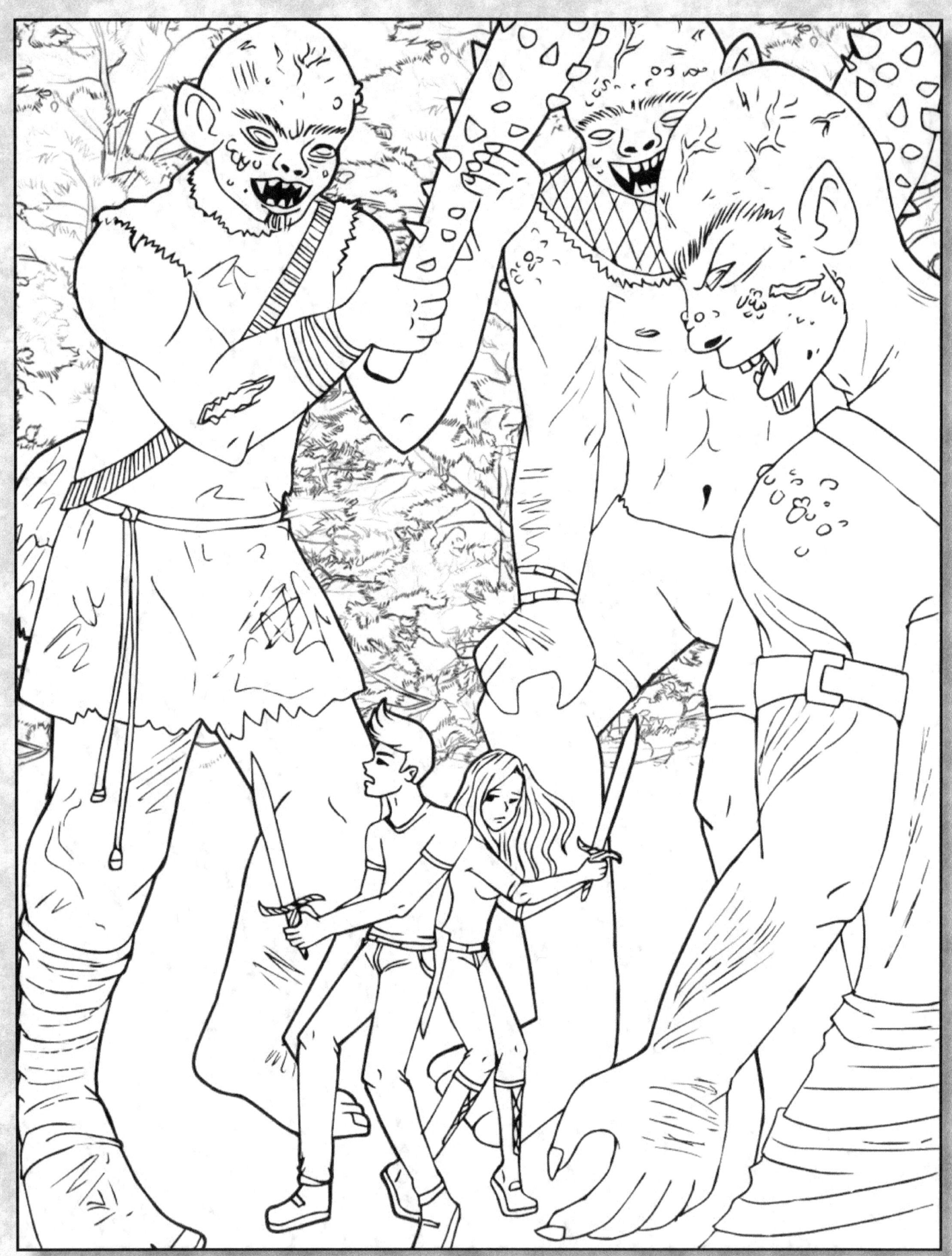

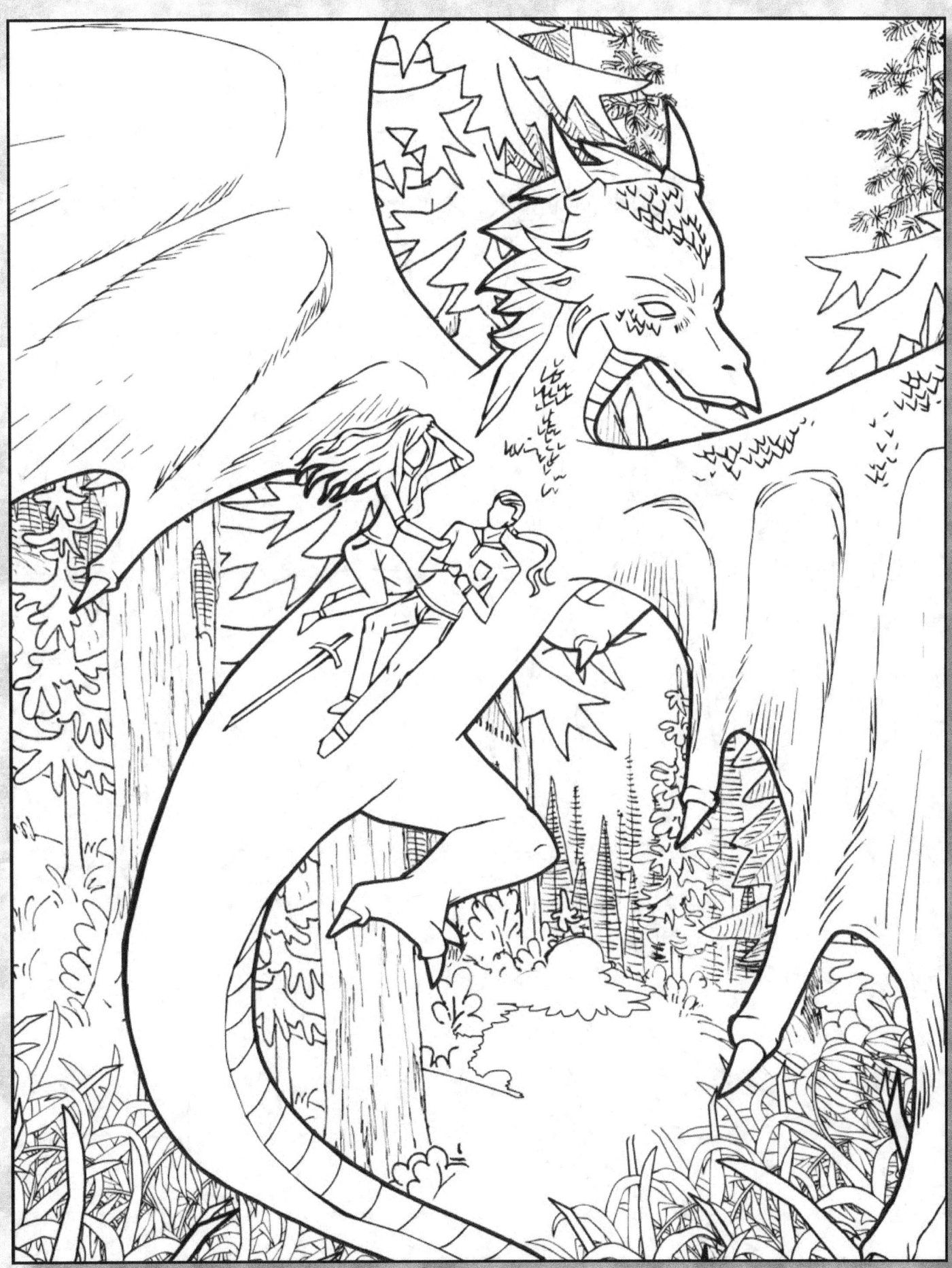

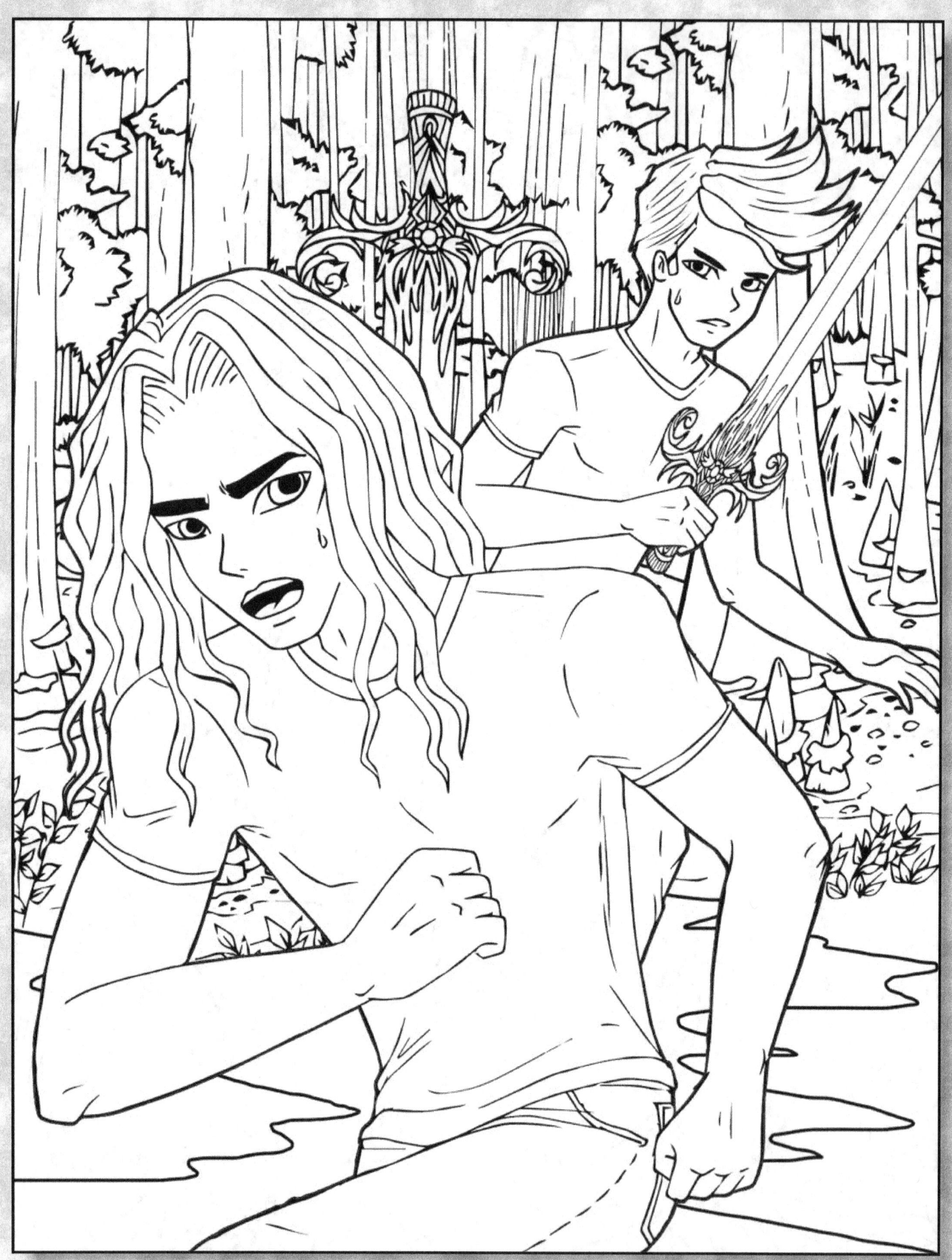

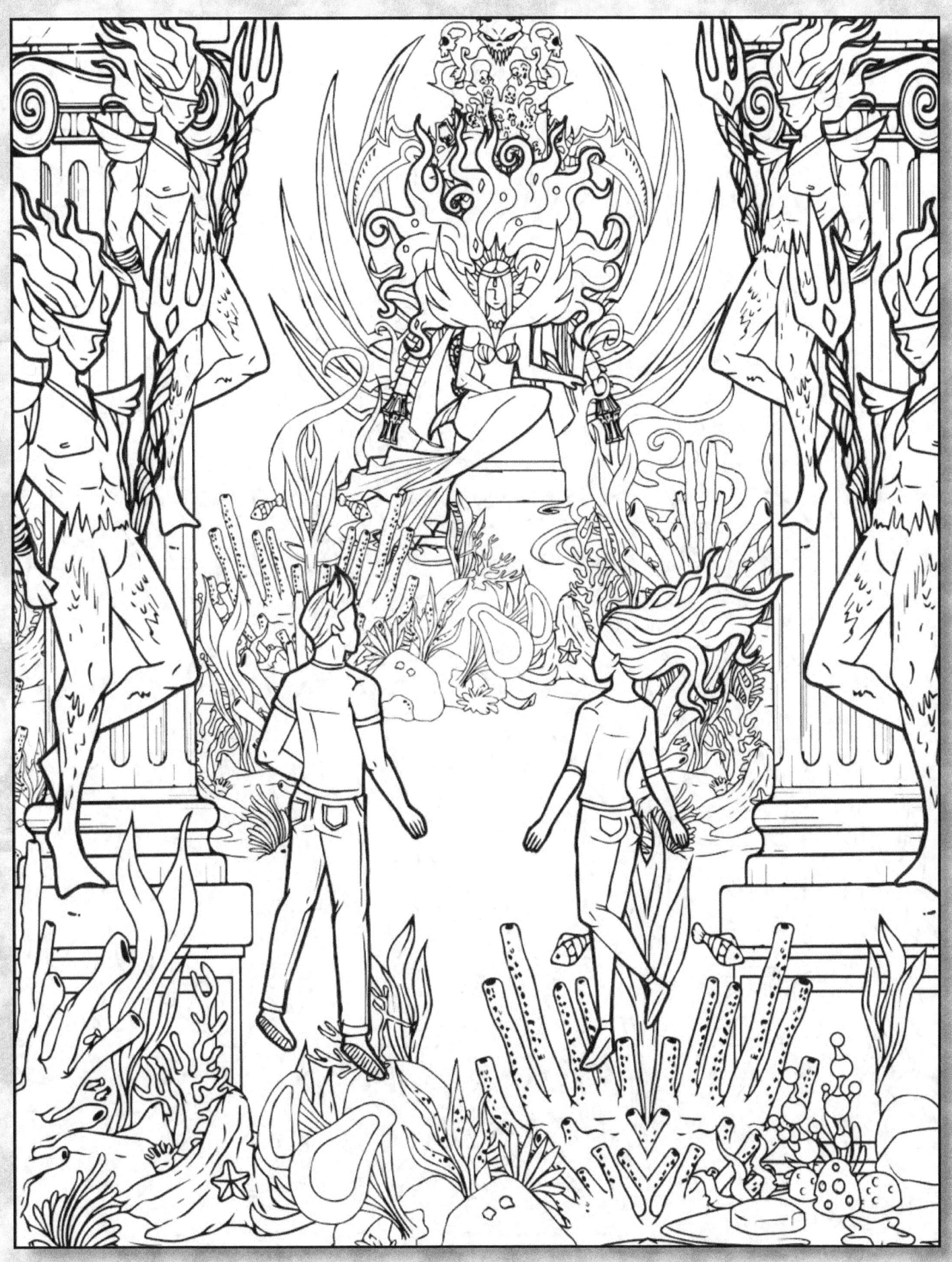

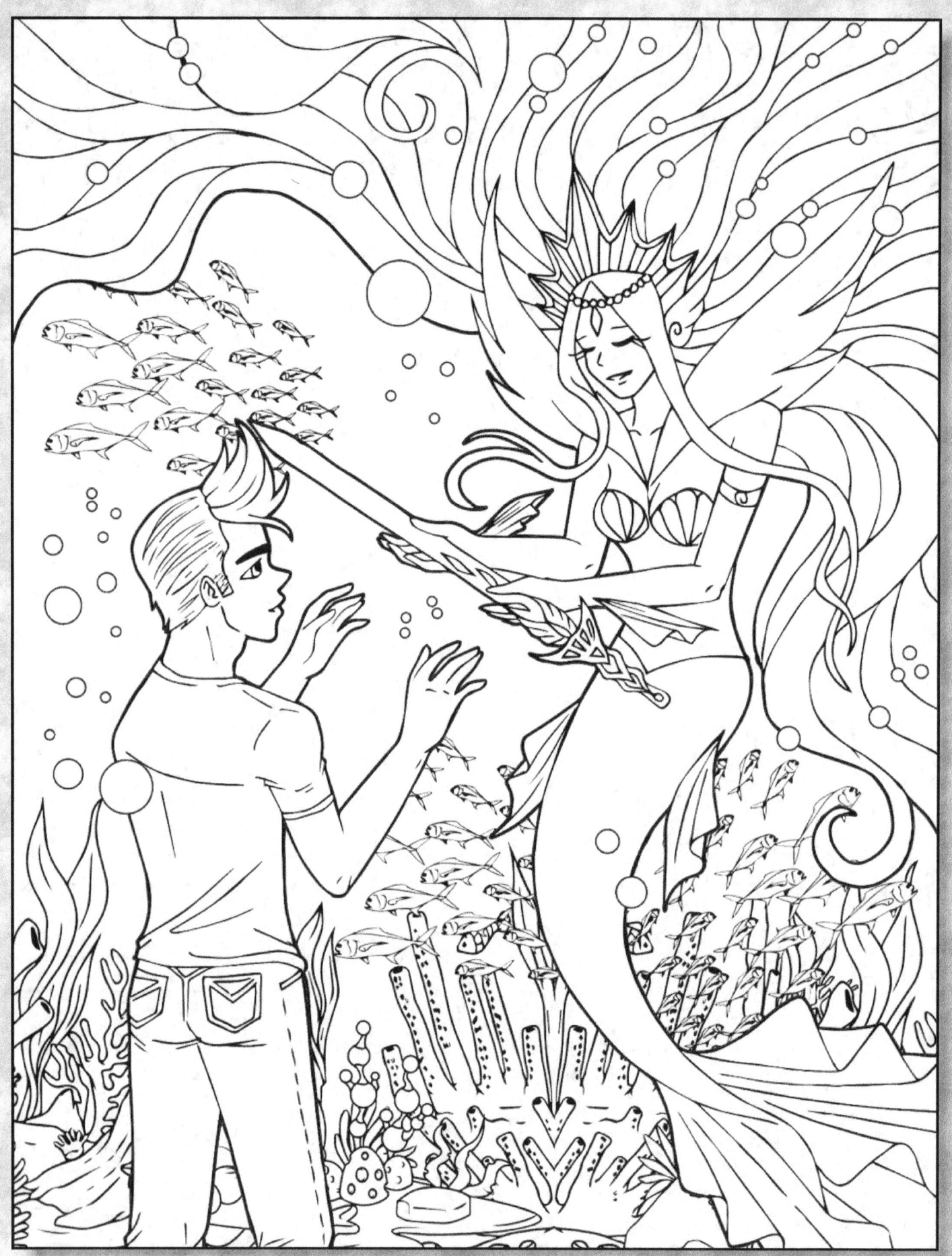

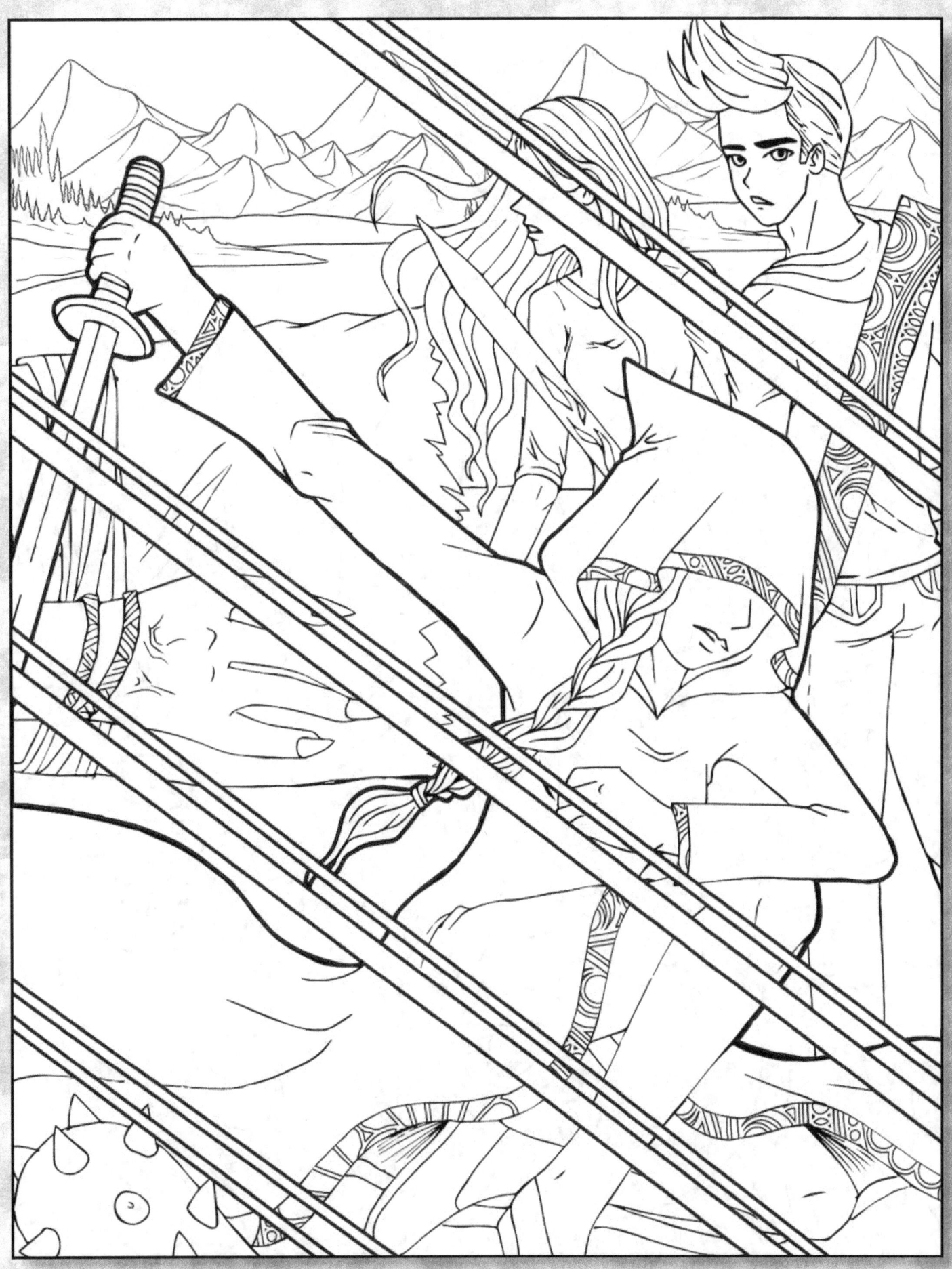

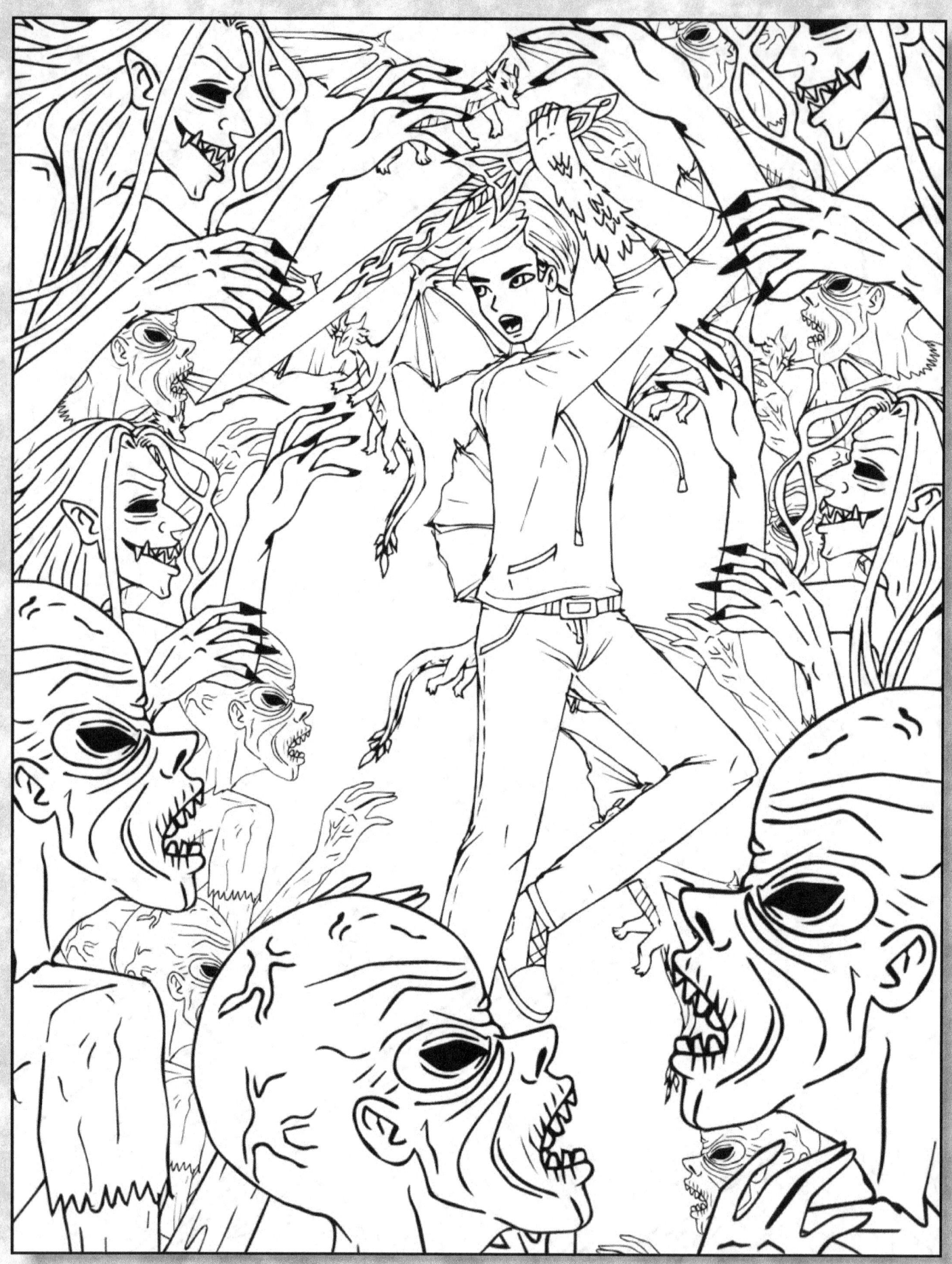

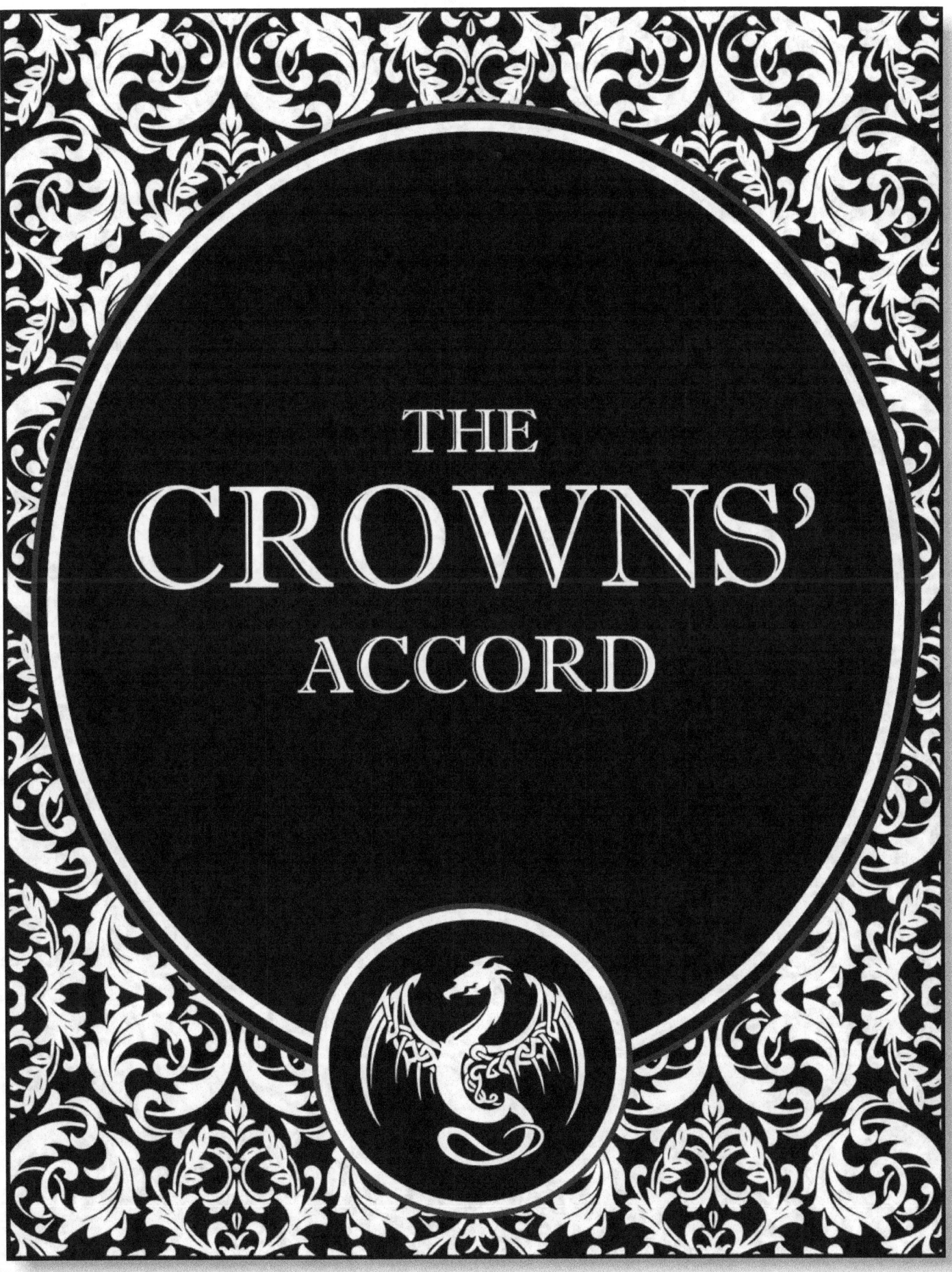

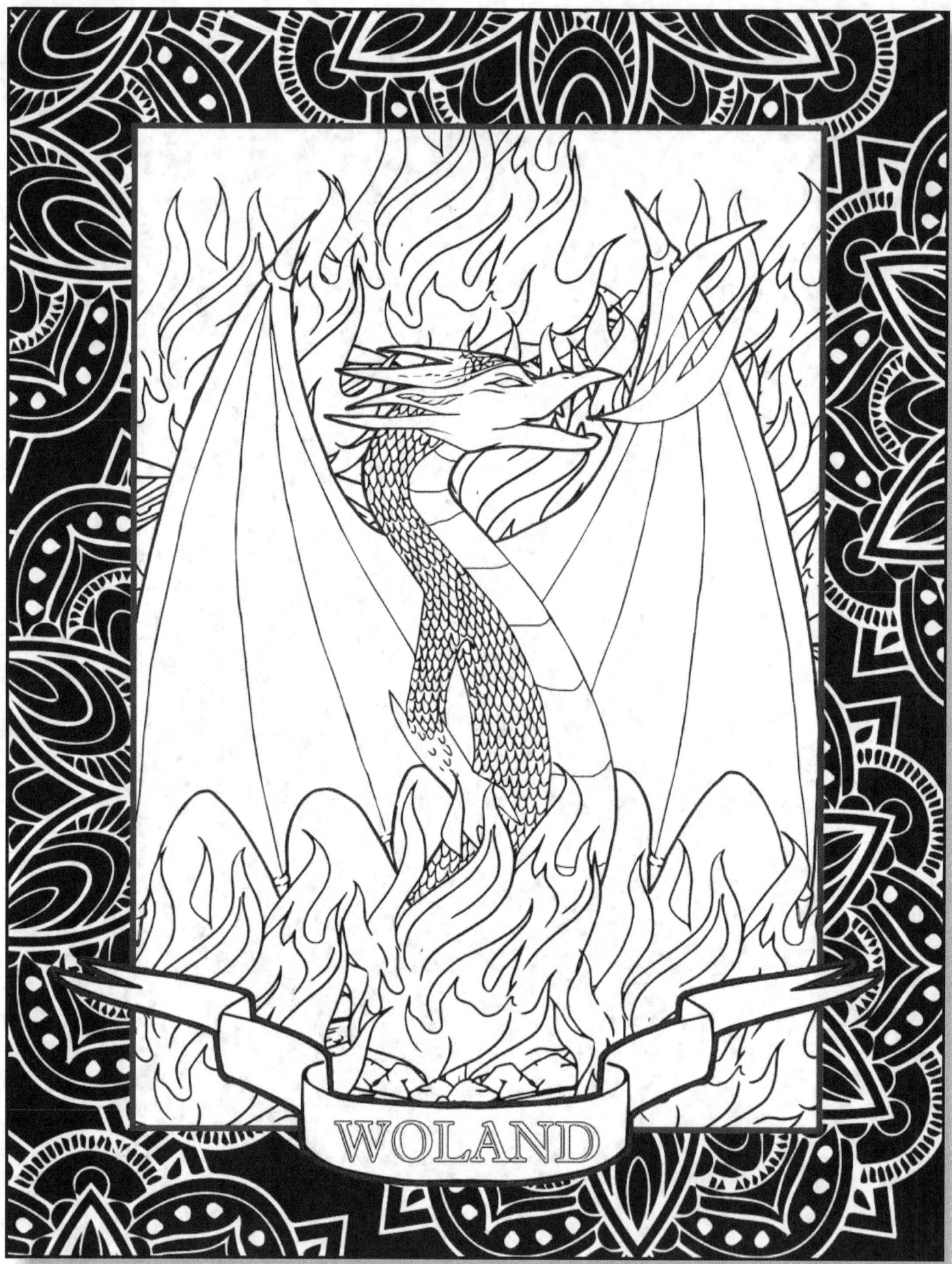

WOLAND

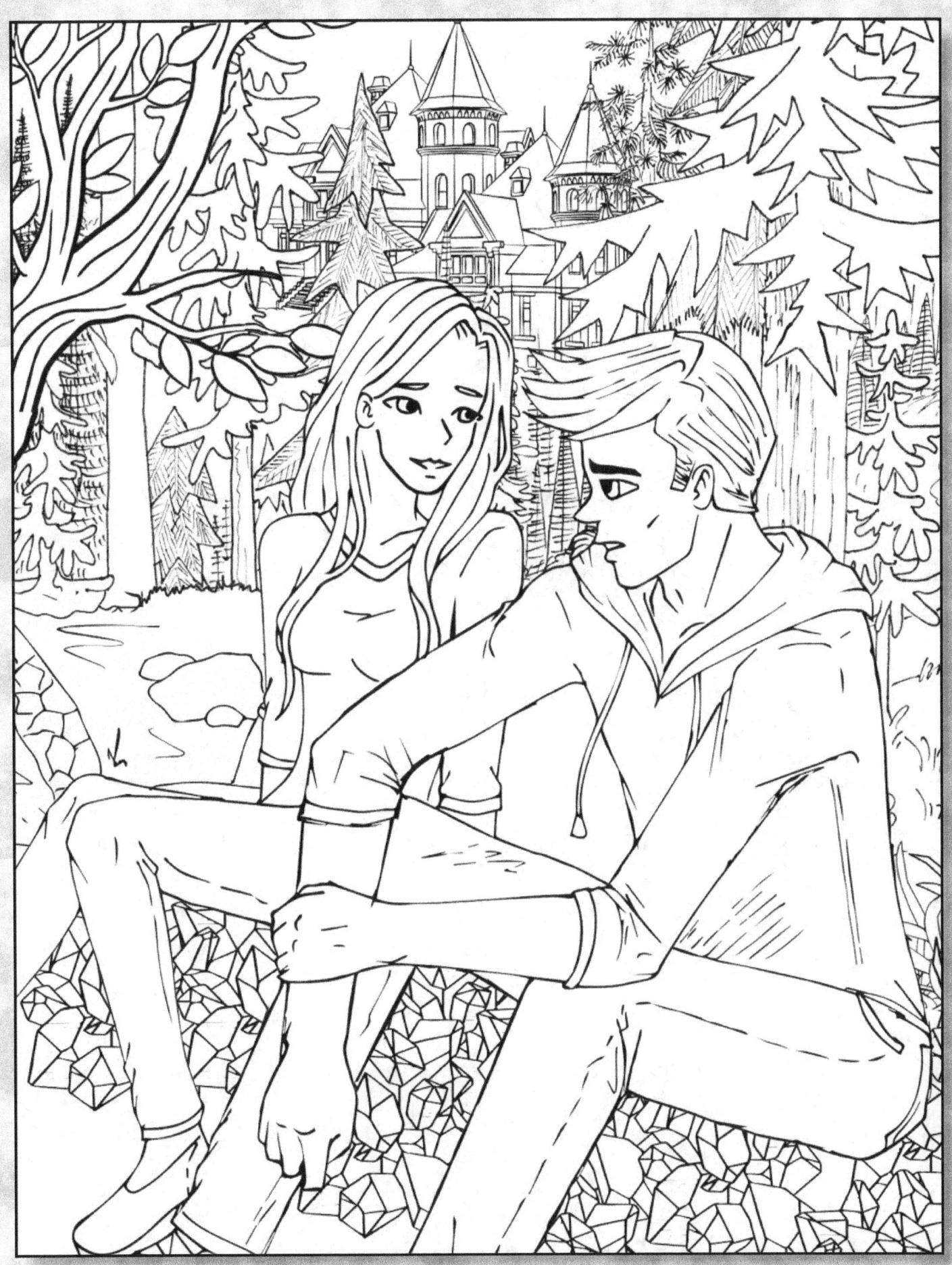

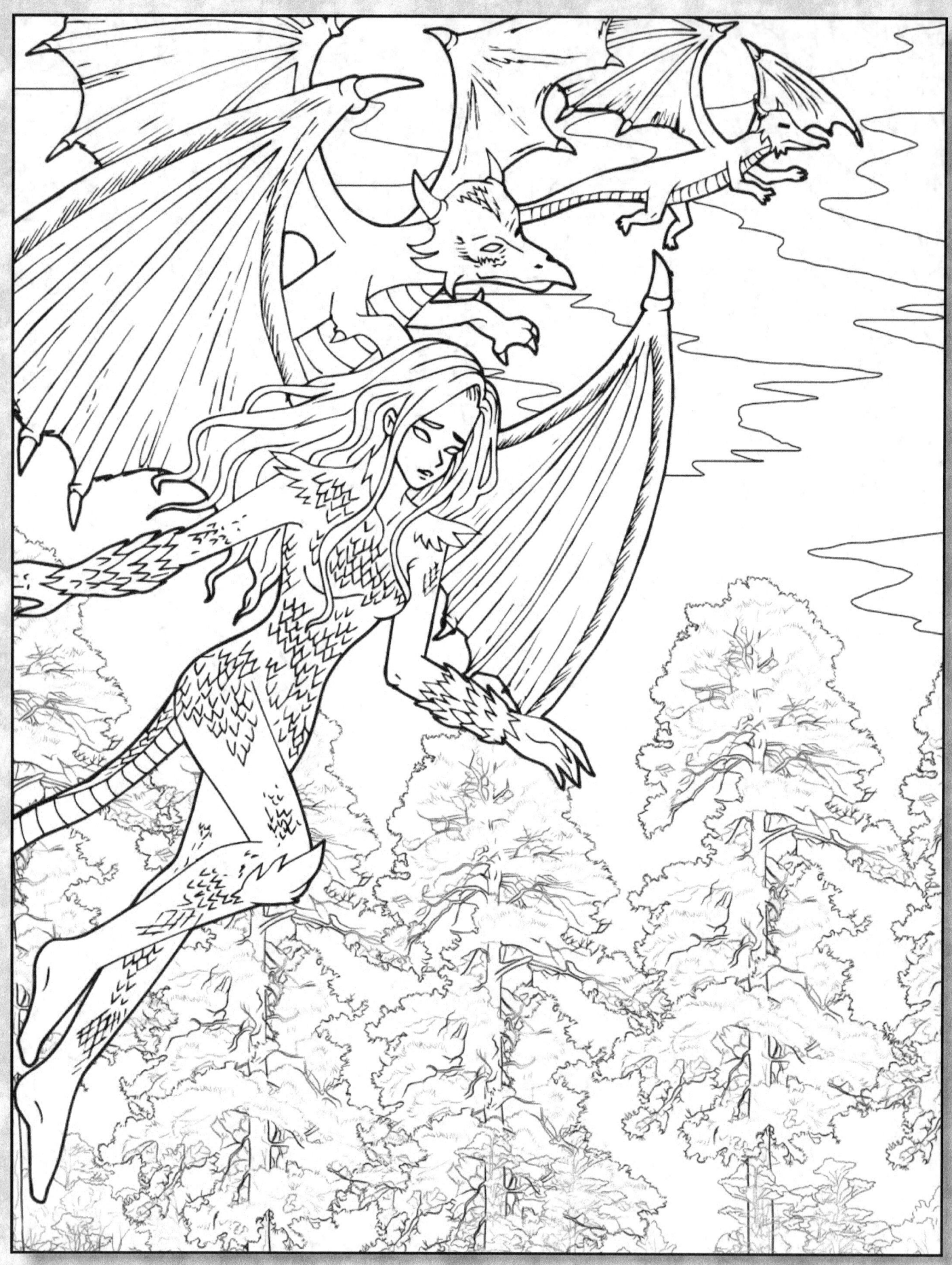

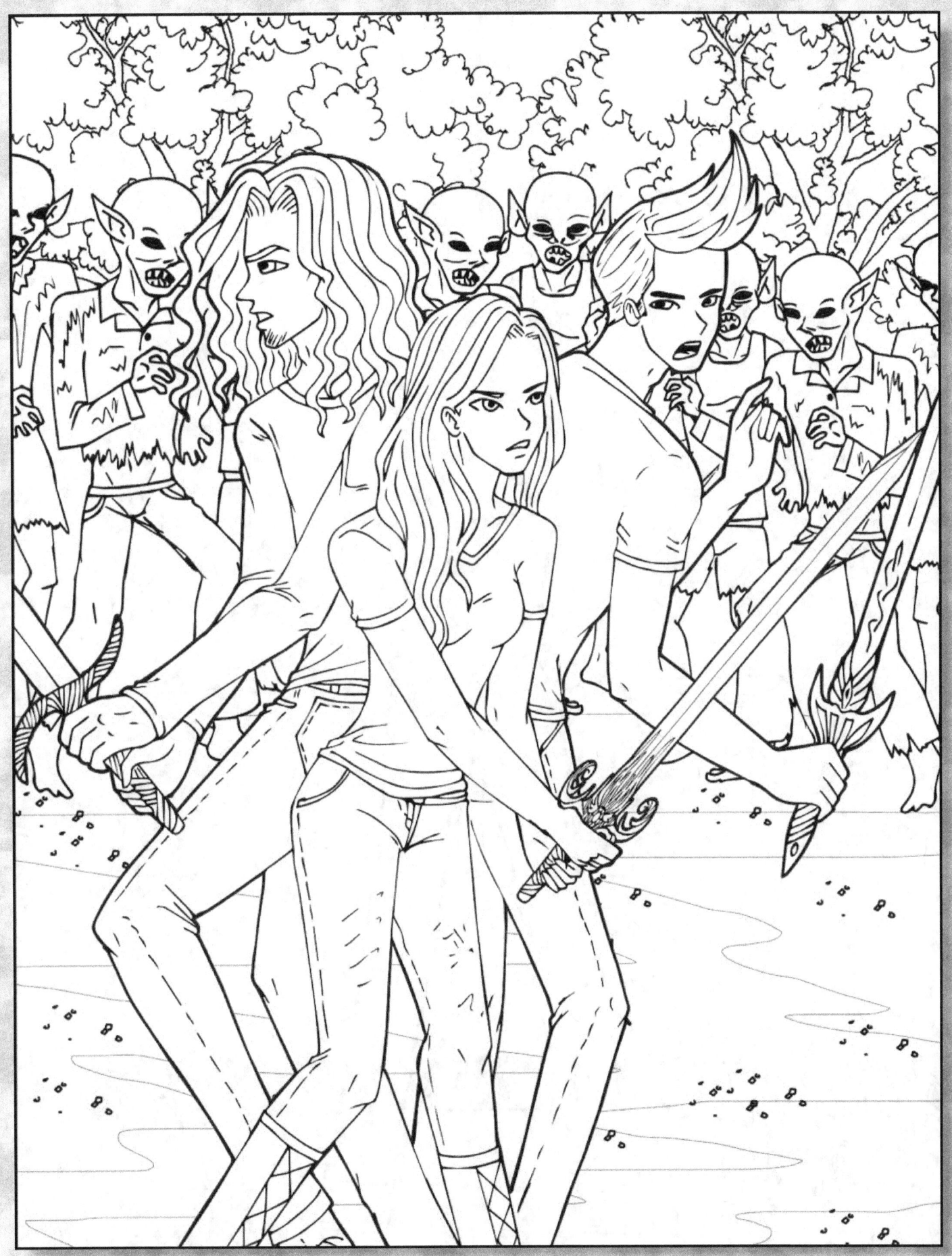

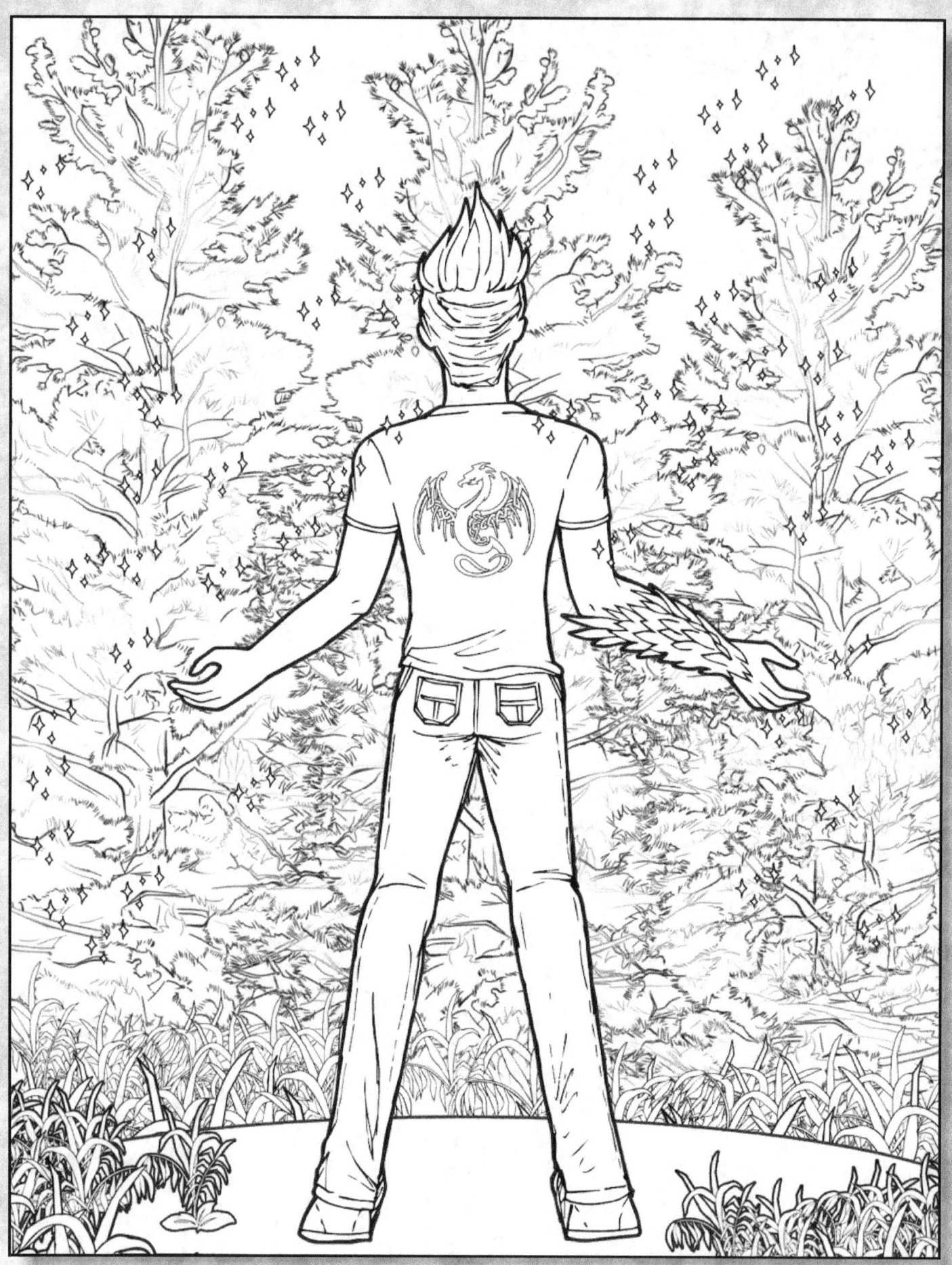

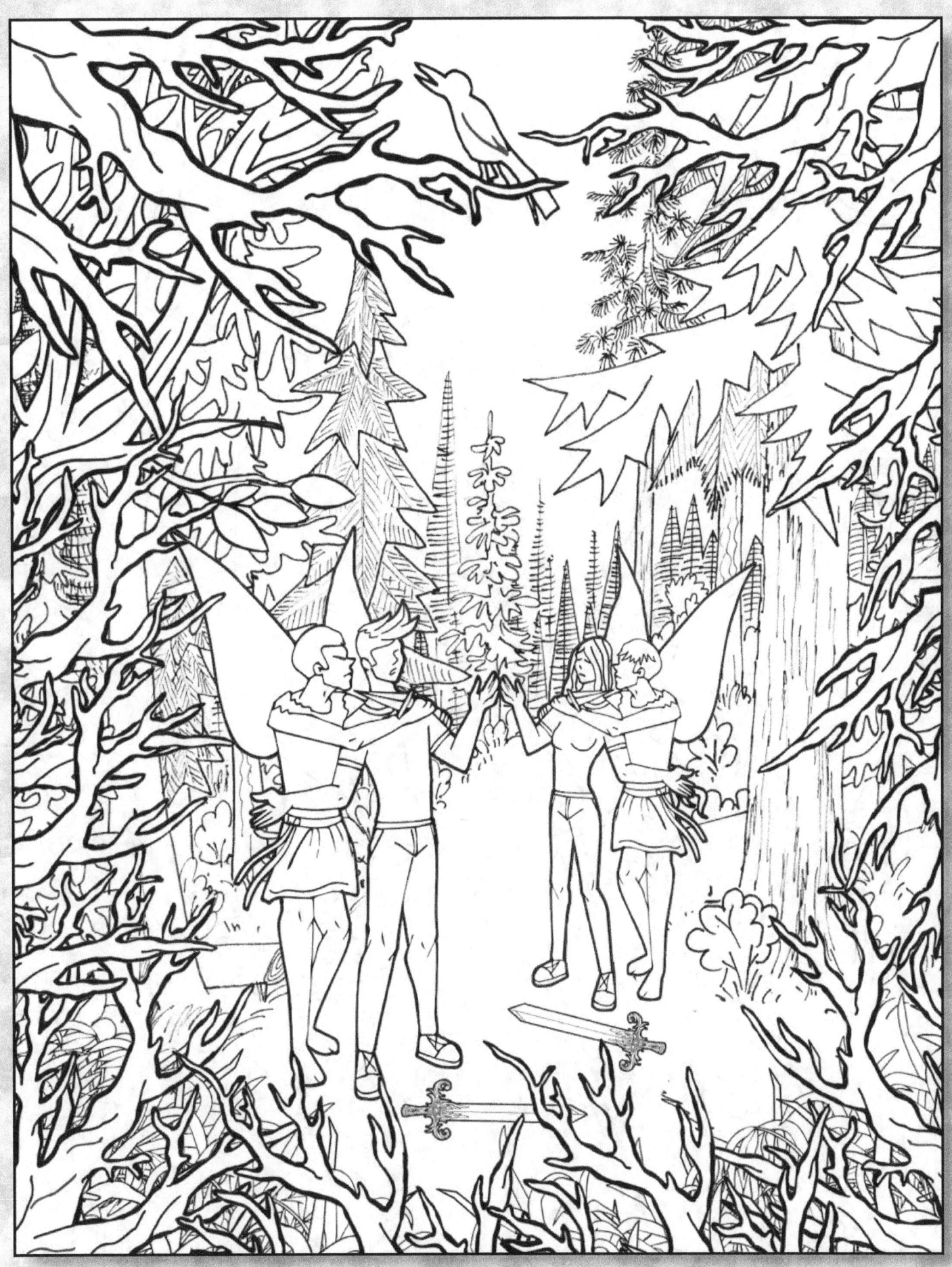

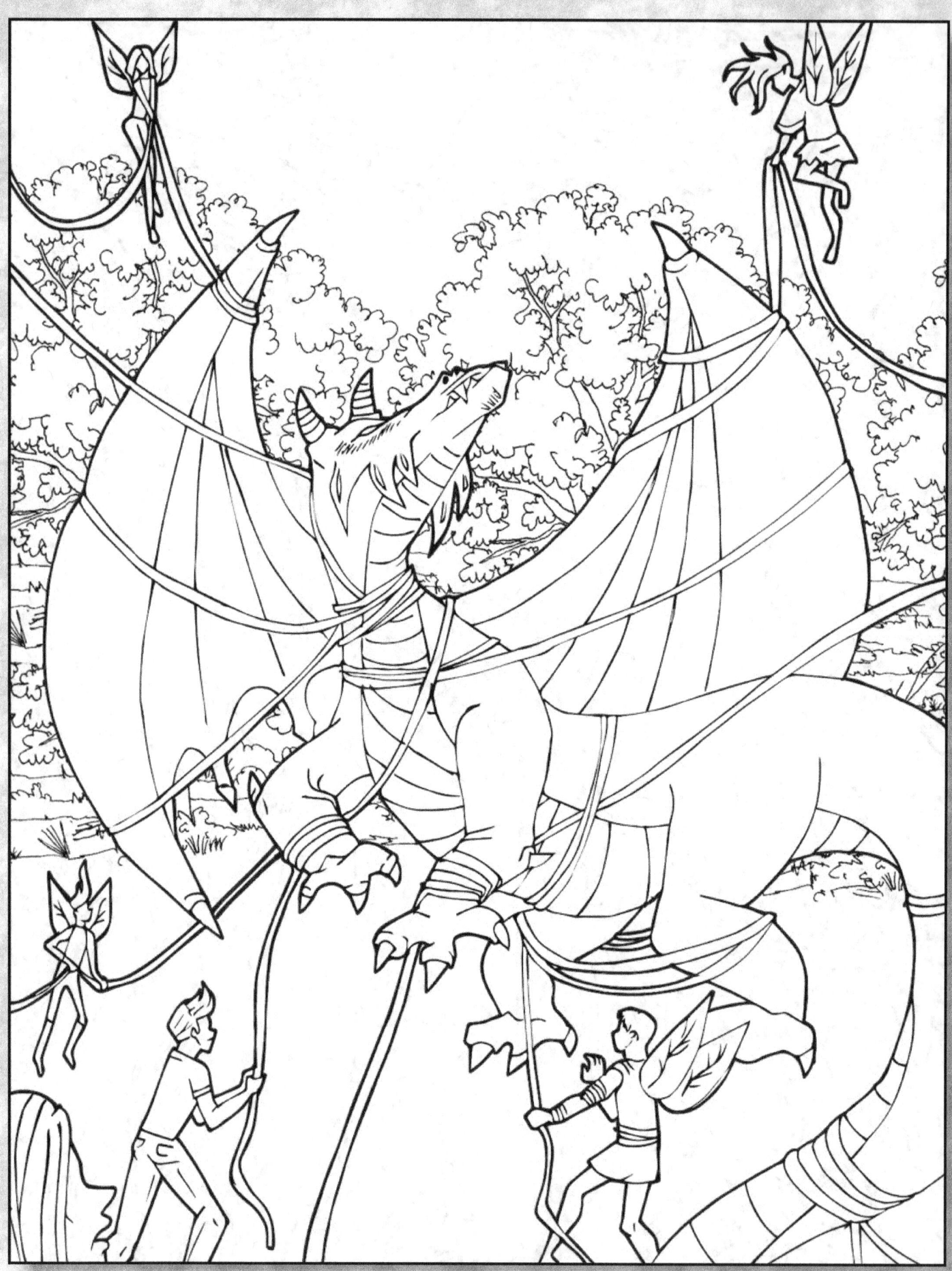

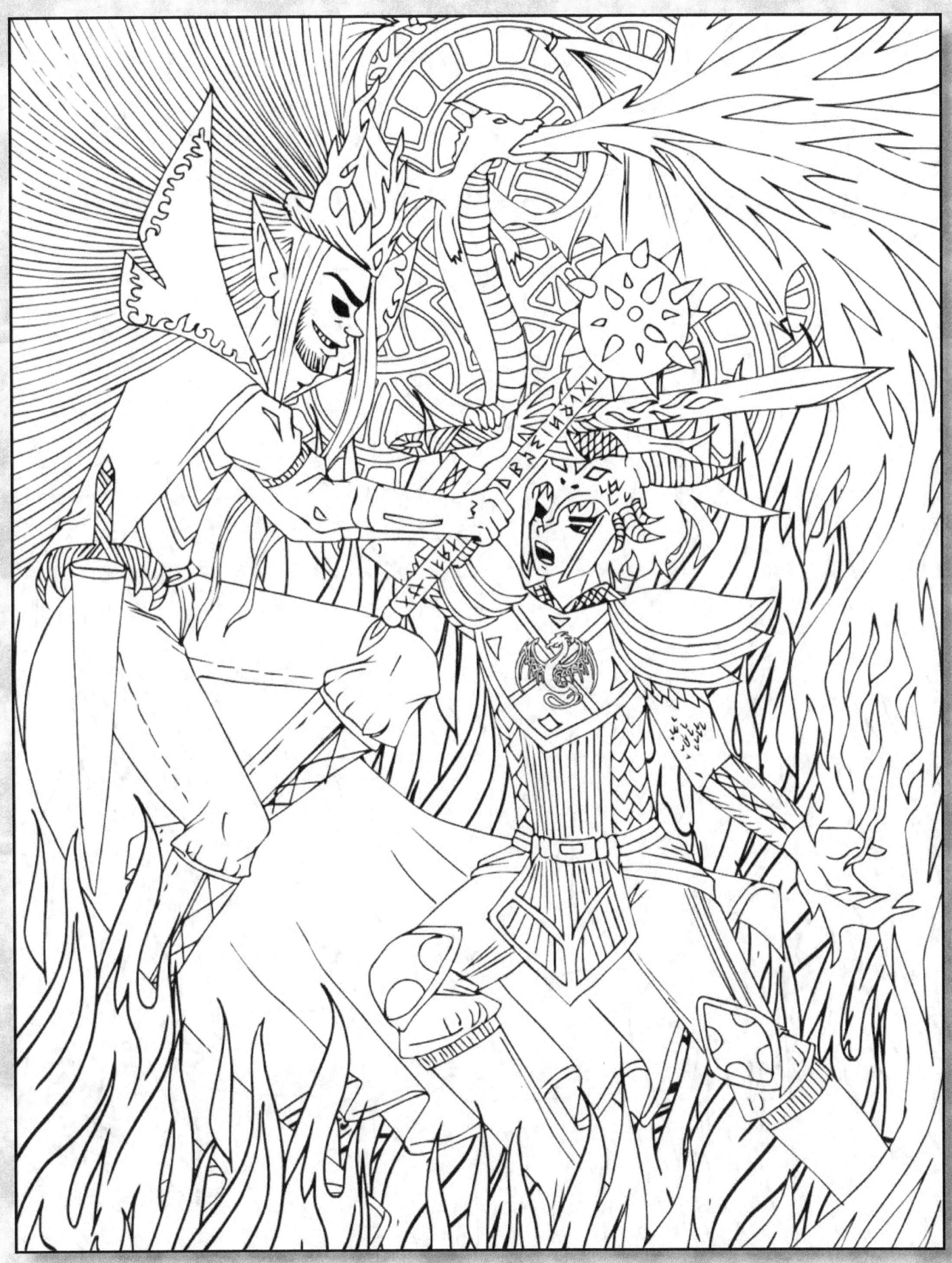

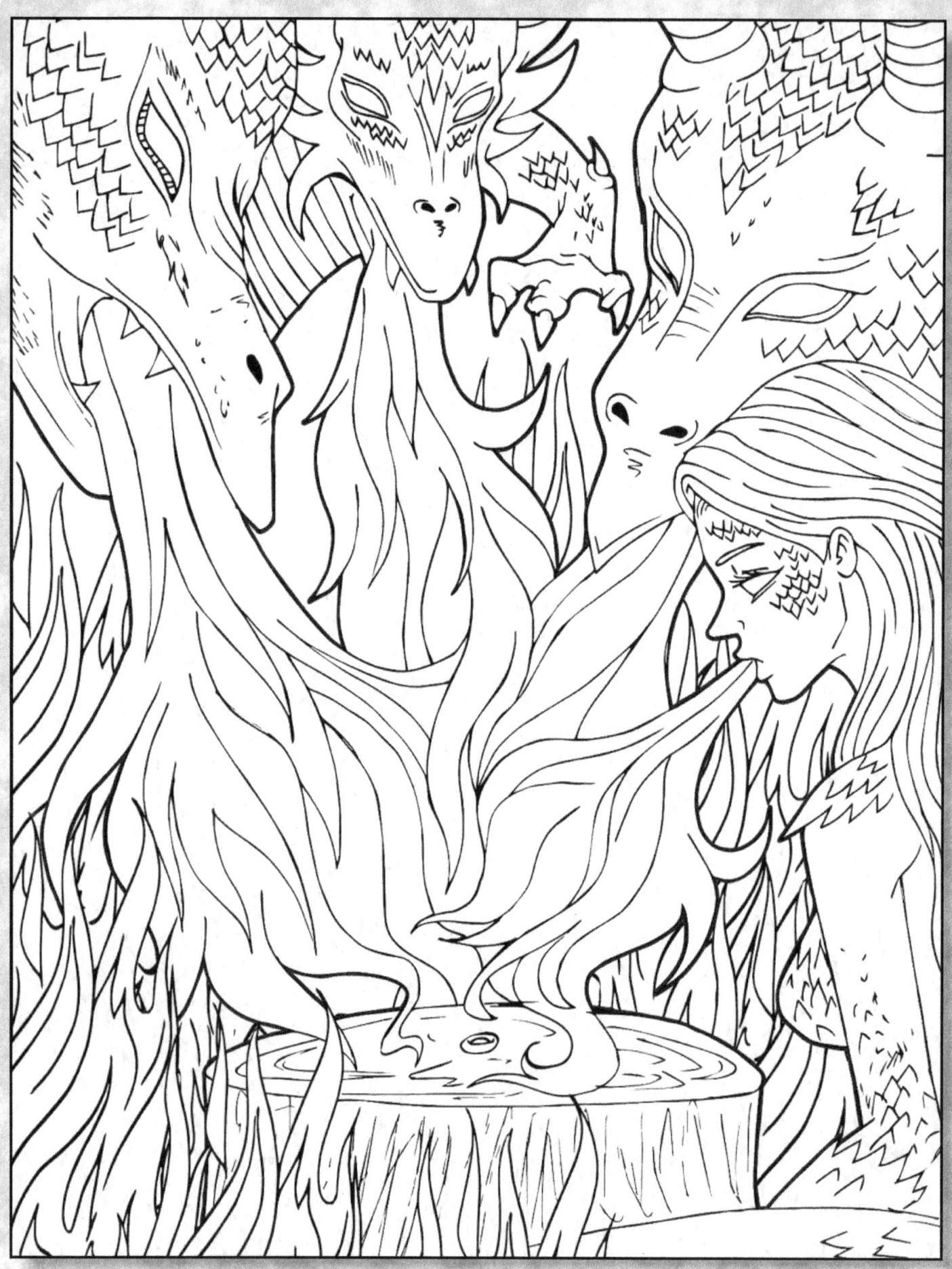

About the Author

J.A. Culican is a USA Today Bestselling author of the middle grade fantasy series Keeper of Dragons. Her first novel in the fictional series catapulted a trajectory of titles and awards, including top selling author on the USA Today bestsellers list and Amazon, and a rightfully earned spot as an international best seller. Additional accolades include Best Fantasy Book of 2016, Runner-up in Reality Bites Book Awards, and 1st place for Best Coming of Age Book from the Indie book Awards.

J.A. Culican holds a Master's degree in Special Education from Niagara University, in which she has been teaching special education for over 13 years. She is also the president of the autism awareness non-profit Puzzle Peace United. J.A. Culican resides in Southern New Jersey with her husband and four young children.

To find out more about the Keeper of Dragons visit:

www.jaculican.com

About the Artist

Arnild Cuarteron Aldepolla is a freelance artist who just can't stop drawing. He is a huge fan of young adult and teen books and can often be found doodling inspirations from anime/manga and Disney. He's the artist behind the coloring book for both teens and adult of some authors including Cameo Renae's Hidden Wings, Shelly Crane's Significance, Randi Cooley Wilson's Revelation, Ednah Walters' Runes and many more. J.A. Culican's Keeper of Dragons is his latest work.

Arnild has a Bachelor of Fine Arts in Visual Communication from PWC, and resides in Davao City, Philippines with his mother. He is currently working on several more coloring books anticipating release next year.

Arnild can be found on
Facebook: arnild.aldepolla
IG: booksandfanarts
and his website
booksandfanartsblog.wordpress.com/AT

He can be reached via email
arncaldepolia@yahoo.com.ph